One

Other Books by Paul F. Gorman

The Miracle Self

The Giving Self

The Impersonal Self

Spiritual Healing of the Mind and Body

The Way of Awakening

Satisfied with God Alone

The 7 Spiritual Steps To Solving Any Problem

Opening The Windows of Heaven

The Fully Manifest Self

Only God Is

That Which You Seek

www.miracleself.com

One

PAUL F. GORMAN

VINE
PRESS

REDONDO BEACH
CALIFORNIA

One

FIRST EDITION 2016

ISBN-13: 978-0692613153

ISBN-10: 0692613153

Published by Vine Press, Redondo Beach, California USA

Set in Original Garamond BT 10/12.5

Printed by CreateSpace

Available worldwide from Amazon and all other
online and traditional book stores.

www.miracleself.com

Edited by M.L.

My everlasting gratitude to you for your unwavering help in making the Miracle Self teachings fit for readers.

Rise in conscious awareness—this is the entire secret.

As conscious awareness rises, detaching from and leaving behind false belief, ever greater degrees of heaven become visible through the unconditioned mind.

“As in heaven so in earth.”

The earth and all its people, creatures and conditions are witnessed unconditioned, whole and harmonious, love and union of all emerging through the fog of false sense.

Indeed, “As in heaven so in earth” emerges as the one reality. The bondage of false, material sense is dispelled, and the unconditioned experience of man, earth and universe is experienced harmonious, peaceful and free, in love.

Paul F. Gorman

CONTENTS

1

I

MILLIONS AROUND THE WORLD struggle with fear, loneliness, lack of purpose, limitation, disease, poverty, starvation, immorality, injustice and depression. Yet, the truth, purpose and freedom of all beings are immediately evident in the consciousness of oneness.

The earth itself is today struggling to breathe amongst the smothering fog of humanity's unawareness and self-indulgence. Yet the beauty, bounty and fulfillment of earth is immediately evident in the consciousness of oneness.

It is time to understand and to awaken to conscious oneness, and in that way "release" the individual, the race as a whole, and the earth to be what all truly are in tangible, visible and real experience.

Let us awaken, and in our awakening see ourselves as we truly are and what we are for; let us experience our earth as what she truly is, and what she is for.

As the light of oneness fills individual consciousness all is known and tangibly seen as harmonious, the "part" being in union with the "whole"—health, love, abundance, peace and fulfillment of purpose real and evident and freely available as all, for all.

Let us lift out of the dream state of struggle, pain and limitation and understand how the miracle of God consciousness dissipates even the most overwhelming problems of humanity and its world—even those which are deemed by those who are "expert" in their field to be fatal disease, disaster or ruin.

THAT WHICH SEEMS TO BE IS NOT THAT WHICH IS

Only that which *is* is truth (reality, God). All "else," all that which appears to be un-God-like—sick, poor, inharmonious, limited, unloving, unfulfilled—is belief; and because all belief seems to be real, our "reality" has seemed to lack God (good).

Let us see how belief proves to have no power in and of its own self, and is dissolved and made as nothing in the light of conscious oneness. Let us, here and now, discover how to stand up and walk free in the tangible experience of that which *is.*

Open yourself to the spirit of the words on these pages. "The words that I speak to you, they are spirit, and they are life. . . . Be still [still your human, corporeal sense], and know that I am God." Be still, and realize that *I,* your *I,* all of *I,* is *God, spirit and truth.*

I has been given many different names over the centuries, but the purest name is simply *I* or *consciousness,* which is God, spirit, truth—the all-inclusive experience (universal formation) of being.

If somehow the *I* of you were taken away, there would be nothing left of you or your universe, not an atom. The *I* of you *is* everything of you; the *I* of you is *one being* your entire universe inclusive of its every form and moment.

You experience your *sense* of *I* (God or spirit); I experience mine. *I* is one or oneness. *I* is consciousness, and consciousness is *omni*presence, *omni*-awareness, *omni*-all.

Even though *I* (consciousness) appears to be an infinite universe that we each exist *within* (and are conscious *of*), being exists inclusive of its universe and all the form its universe constitutes. *I is one, all* and *omnipresent.*

To belief it appears as if *I* is buried deep within being, that mind is "in" the head or the brain, that life exists "in" the body, and that the self I am exists "in" the world which in turn exists "in" the universe. This is how existence *seems* to be, but what it truly is is *I, consciousness, spirit—one.*

Our entire being, mind, body and universe, our every moment of experience and every form of it, are one (God). What seem to be I "and" experience are not I "and," but I *being* the totality of experience.

"All things were made by him; and without him was not any thing made that was made. . . . He was in the world, and the world was made by him, and the world knew him not. . . . And God saw every thing that he had made, and, behold, it was very good."

God is the only, the all-in-all and all-of-all, and God is spirit not matter—incorporeality not corporeality. Corporeality is simply our *sense* of that which is one hundred percent incorporeal: God. With this understanding, we see that all formation, all of experience, all of the universe, all of infinity and omnipresence; all being, mind, body, thing, amount, place and condition are *spirit,* not matter; incorporeal, not corporeal.

Everything everywhere of me, every detail and form of my experience, is spirit and spiritual—one.

All is God, which is spirit. The I that I am is the I that God is because there is none but God. The universe I experience is the universe I am being, which is God being all.

I am spiritual being, spiritual mind and spiritual body. My universe, my world, and everything everywhere in and of my experience is spirit. Every activity, amount and place; every breath and every step; every sound, color and fragrance are spirit. Because all is spirit, all is whole and complete—one, self-complete, self-contained and self-governed.

Hear it deeply: because all is spirit, all is *one.* God or spirit is one, not many; is indivisible, inseparable, unalterable as only one can be. If spirit consisted of two or more, then, of course, the two or more could easily become divided and separated, different from each other.

God or spirit is one, and because God is all, *I* am that. The entirety of individual being and experience *is that one,* infinite, omnipresent, indivisible and inseparable, existent as its entirety at every point of itself at the same time.

"I and the Father are one." The Father is oneness, omnipresence, the whole of itself equally and fully alive and present everywhere at the same time, *spirit,* not matter.

I am spirit; my mind is spirit, my universe and everything everywhere in it and of it are spirit. Therefore, that which I am aware of and think about and experience is SPIRIT*—*SPIRITUAL *beings, things, places and conditions.*

Nothing but spirit exists. Spirit is one, omnipresence, all. Spirit is what we *are,* what we are aware *with,* and what we are aware *of.*

The miracle of truth is that even as we believe we are thinking about human, physical, material, structural "reality," we are not. None of these exist in God, in spirit. "I am the Lord, and besides me there is none else." The beliefs we have had about matter are actually about spirit and spiritual things because only spirit exists, and only spirit is *aware.*

Life, *I,* is all-inclusive oneness. The universe of being and experience is one, not two, not a multitude, and that one is spirit, the incorporeal, forever whole, complete and in perfect order. *I live and move and have my being in an infinite ocean of God or spirit or oneness.* The "I" I believe I am—the "I" that is living and moving and having its being "in" God—is itself God existing as individual and unique "me" and "my" universal experience along with individual and unique "everyone else" and "their" universal experience.

We are each the whole of God, spirit, experiencing—*being*—the one infinite entirety of existence. And because God is good without opposite, all of existence is good without opposite. "God saw that everything he had made was very good. . . . The earth [formation, experience] is full of the goodness of the Lord." Existence and its experience are full of the goodness of the Lord, of spirit, of oneness. I am that one, you are that one, all is that one.

But what are our thoughts about when we struggle with a problem? Are they about the reality of spirit, God, oneness, infinity and omnipresence, the immediate fulfillment of the God (good) experience? Or are they about the "reality" of the problem, the threat it poses to us, our family, home or business, and its many consequences?

REALITY VERSUS BELIEF

That which is *believed to be* is not that which *is.* Drop the belief in the name and nature, the "reality" of the problem *and* its believed solution. Drop *all* belief and hear truth;

open yourself to reality itself. "Son, you are ever with me, and all that I have is yours." What is it that *I, God,* am and have, therefore what you are and have, and what all is and has?

I am one as you, which includes your experience. *I* am *being* oneness as you and for you. *I* am spirit and truth, and *I* have—*I* am *being*—spirit and truth as you and for you; as all and for all.

There is no name or condition in God. There is nothing but God in God, and because God is all, there is nothing but God in *and happening as* all.

God is one, and full of oneness; therefore all is one and full of oneness—harmony, wholeness, completeness, perfection.

God is one and omnipresent. No person, place, amount or condition has more or less or no God in it. God is all and is fully present as all. God is the one omni-being, omni-place, omni-amount, omni-condition, omni-existence, omni-entity.

God cannot be personalized, localized or finitized. God cannot be "used" for personal gain or for physical or material transformation. God cannot be experienced personally, locally or finitely; nor can God heal matter. If such an act were possible God would have to be both spirit and matter, truth and untruth, light and dark.This belief is nonsense. God is God alone—spirit and truth alone.

God *is.* "He perfects that which concerns me." The almighty, God, spirit, oneness, perfects that which concerns me. "He performs that which I am given to do." He harmonizes, makes perfect and complete that which presents itself to me, or fulfills that which is demanded of me. He performs it. He reveals the truth, the life, the abundance, the peace of that which presents itself to me, as the fulfillment it truly *is.*

"I" IS, AND FULFILLS EXPERIENCE

When we withdraw money from the bank, the bank performs and fulfills the withdrawal for us. Our only involvement is that of *identifying ourselves truthfully* to the bank teller or ATM. As long as we are recognized, our withdrawal is performed and perfected for us. Bringing the same principle to bear, as we realize that we and our entire experience (every detail and form of it, whether good or bad in appearance) *are spirit;* and as we turn to spirit itself *as spiritual being*—ignoring that which seems to be—and simply resting receptively in spirit, we discover that spirit performs and perfects our experience *for us.* We have correctly identified ourselves and so our "withdrawal"—fulfillment—is complete.

No problem or solution is what it seems to be, but is false sense or mis-identity. We mis-identify by believing in an existence or condition other than God. It doesn't matter what name we give to the problem—ill health, disease, lack, limitation, immorality, injustice, unhappiness, poverty, insecurity, homelessness, starvation, or what name we give to their opposites—their solutions. Both the problem and its solution are collectively believed conditions out-pictured or out-formed and believed to be real. But they have no reality, law or principle to uphold them or sustain them in the presence of spirit.

Where a problem seems to be, what its nature seems to be, what its apparent reality seems to be, and what the consequences of that apparent reality seem to be, are actually the presence of oneness, God. All the bad and the good, the problem and the solution of the appearing condition are false sense or mis-identity. That which *actually is*—everywhere and as all formation throughout mind, body and world—is *spirit,* forever whole, complete and perfect.

God's universe is in perfect order, and God's universe is the one and only. But to tangibly experience (have) the perfect order of every person, place, thing and condition we must realize that we and our universe are *that—spirit* and *spiritual.* The order (truth) of our experience is visible and tangible only as we identify ourselves and our universe truthfully—as being God, spirit, oneness. Whether belief presents us with a good or bad person or condition, we must know the truth: all is God, spirit, forever whole and complete, despite appearance.

God is perfect order; belief is perfect disorder.

God is eternal, invariable, real and certain; belief is temporal, unreal and uncertain.

God is principle, ever the same; belief is perverse, ever-changing.

What about the problem you face today? What is it that concerns you? What is its nature, its quality, its disposition? What is it you would like to see perfected, harmonized, healed? Is your health troubling you? Your finances, your relationship, your ability to succeed and enjoy prosperity and freedom of creative expression?

Are these experiences spiritual? They *are. All* experience is spiritual; all form and condition are spirit because nothing but spirit exists. But what do *we believe* a problem or its solution to be? This question begins to open our awareness to truth, to the *principle of oneness,* and to the healing of any and every problem.

What do we believe good to be? What do we believe bad to be? Do we believe these opposites to be real in and of their own selves? Do we believe in God "and"? Do we believe disease, lack, limitation, aversion, poverty, injustice, immorality, insecurity, unhappiness or depression to be realities, principled negative or destructive conditions?

All people, including those who have turned to God or spirit for their and their world's good, experience both good *and* bad. No human beings have only good in their lives. Some struggle with types of problems we do not experience; we struggle with types of problems others do not experience. All such experiences are aspects of *belief* unwittingly accepted as being real. They have nothing to do with God or reality. If we believe that life consists of pairs of opposites, good and bad, we have God "and," and because belief and experience are one, good *and bad* fill our experience.

All truth students probably believe that God, buried deep within, is their ultimate reality. But most *also* believe in the here-and-now reality of disease, poverty, lack, limitation, aversion, danger, insecurity, greed, cruelty, injustice, immorality, unhappiness. *At their own level of sense* these, and the myriad of other problems people suffer, are experienced as being real, and they have real and sometimes devastating effect. But by accepting these and any of the pairs of opposites at their own level we have divided our "house"—our consciousness. We have accepted a belief in God "and." We have made "false idols" from collective belief, and we suffer by them, often racked with fear about what "bad" will do to us.

Fear, pain and suffering are caused by our seeming separation from God. We cannot find God anywhere among the pairs of opposites, not even among their good. Yes, even good *when good is believed to be real in and of its own self* has nothing to do with God, and cannot evidence God.

In belief, this is why good can turn to bad—sometimes overnight. God seems to be different and separate from us and we from God. God seems to be unreachable, unattainable, unreal and impractical even to the majority of students on the path seeking. Why?

First, to those who are suffering, who seem to have no way out, whose problem seems to be insurmountable, be assured that God is fully present with you and as you and as all in your life this minute. At every moment God is fully present and openly available. Rest in this assurance; rest the weary mind; cease believing you need do battle with that which seems to be. This very moment God *is being* you and everything of your experience.

Rest and begin to *feel* this truth. Begin to feel the truth that God is real, and that because God is real God is practical. The truth is that God is the *one* and *only* existence, therefore the one and only real and practical life. Only *belief* leaves us and our experience (*in sense,* never in reality) separate and apart from God—from our good, purpose and freedom of being.

If you could roll out your mind on a dining table, as if it were a large scroll, and take a look at everything going on in it, what would you discover? What combination of good and bad fills your mind? How many thousands of beliefs have taken lodging in you—even beliefs about God? How many thoughts about everything *but God* do you entertain? How many have you entertained this month, this day, *this hour?* What have you entertained since you woke up this morning? How many belief-thoughts rather than God-thoughts have you unwittingly allowed to run rampant in you?

It is shocking to discover the un-God-like state of our awareness when we pause to examine ourselves.

Recent neuro-imaging experiments have revealed that the average person has between 50,000 - 70,000 thoughts in each 24 hour period—up to around 2900 per hour. These numbers are not published in a scientific journal, but they make the point. We each have many thousands of different thoughts throughout the day. How many of them are about God versus the personal self, body, loved ones, money, business; fears, needs or desires?

Being aware of our thousands of thoughts helps us keep guard at the gate of our minds. We must become master guards, honoring and protecting our spiritual selves from the barrage of collective belief. We must keep alive in us the truth that, *despite appearance,* only God is, that our entire existence and every form of it is God and none else.

Appearance presents us with a variety of good and bad; every day we observe healthy and unhealthy people, rich and poor people, satisfying and dissatisfying conditions. We must, despite these appearances, keep ourselves filled with a living awareness of God being the only actual presence and reality. We must detach and withdraw from all that appears to be and live in God awareness.

We all know that the good things and conditions of life can, either gradually or out of the blue, turn bad. The reason they can is that everything of the self and world that we have accepted as being real in and of its own self, is not reality but *belief;* and every belief has an opposite.

The self and world that we have believed to be real are unreal. They are unwittingly accepted collective belief about that which is *actual:* God. Because we have believed that which appears to be, our existence has been filled with a never-ending combination of opposites—good and bad. This is why good can and often does turn bad, and equally why bad can be turned to good.

One day or year can be filled with love, happiness, success, prosperity and security; the next can turn to aversion, unhappiness, failure, lack or insecurity. Then, by great mental and physical effort, we can solve the bad and again experience good. The cycle is endless, and the effort required to find solutions for every problem is ever more demanding and exhausting.

Every human being experiences this cycle, at least in some measure; and until our dissatisfaction, pain and suffering eventually drive us to God, we remain imprisoned with no real and lasting answers available. As we finally turn to God and discover that the root of all good and bad is belief, and that, because God is all, belief has no actuality, no law or principle to uphold it, we are close to freedom.

2

A SPIRITUAL STATE OF BEING

WE ARE IMPRISONED BY and suffer from belief alone. We unwittingly prevent ourselves from experiencing the freedoms and joys of truth only by our continuing *belief* that that which presents itself to us—both good and bad—is real *in and of its own self.* Only belief prevents us from dismissing appearance and immediately evidencing God (good without opposite) as all.

As we awaken to the truth of the oneness and omnipresence of God and refuse to continue to believe that anything is different from God, we emerge into our freedom. As Shakespeare's character, Hamlet, states, "There is nothing either good or bad, but thinking [belief] makes it so." There is nothing either good or bad, but belief makes it *appear to be so.* Belief fills our experience with its image and likeness, its formation; and even though all belief-form is imagery alone (imagery without law or principle to uphold or sustain it), as long as appearing formation is believed to be real, it acts as reality. The moment God is realized to be all, and we cease from belief, our experience is released and we and our world quickly become free. Our bodies, worlds and activities become filled with tangible, real God experience.

All is God. Nothing seemingly good or bad has reality. Only God is reality. All that *seem to be* are concepts, temporal forms of belief; unreality accepted as real.

The human (mental, physical, material) realm of awareness is not what it is believed to be, but is God. Only God is, only spirit is, only the incorporeal is, only one is.

Even thought, both good and bad, is God because only God is. We *interpret* thought (just as we interpret everything from a state of belief) as being either good or bad, but if God is infinite, therefore all, then all thought too is God.

That which appears to be matter (corporeal), including thought, is simply our *sense* or *interpretation* of God or spirit (the incorporeal). God, the incorporeal, is the only; God is the all-in-all and all-of-all. Nothing is good or bad; all is God. The corporeal realm of awareness is simply God sensed as matter, but sense does not change reality. Our sensed experience is actually God and "full of the goodness of God." Sense and its formation are innocent and impotent, good without opposite.

Only belief clouds the pure good that we and our world are. In most scriptures, belief is named "the devil." Belief is indeed devilish because in the realm of belief God is nowhere to be found. God is not, and cannot be persuaded to be, evident in belief. Belief cannot be helped by God. If you have wondered why praying to God, filling your mind full of God, meditating and sitting in silence to heal, pacify, prosper or harmonize a human or material condition fails to "work," this is why.

"Ye ask, and receive not, because ye ask amiss."

Recognize belief to be what it is—a lie, "the father of lies," an unwittingly accepted deceit, a falsity which leaves us with a foggy or mis-identified experience of ourselves and our world. Awaken to the one truth, the one reality, which is that God is all. Realize that only God is; only *one* is, and that *one* is the infinite, the omnipresent, the whole and perfect all, the eternally fulfilled one that *is* life, *is* form, *is* all.

"I and the Father are one." I and God are one because only God is. I and form are one; form and I are one. I, mind, body, world and universe, and everything in and of it, are *one,* not many, not different, not separate, not isolated and alone, not of good and bad, but of God *alone.*

There is no good versus bad being; there is only God, therefore only God-being. There is no good versus bad form; there is only God-form. There is no good versus bad world, place, activity, thing, amount or condition; there is *only God.* There is not even a good belief versus a bad; there is *only God.* All "else" is false sense alone, accepted as reality by a believer.

Do not be a believer. All is God, and God is not good or bad; God is only God, and is full of God, and is the very universal form of God. God *is*—period. Nothing corporeal exists; existence is incorporeal (God, spirit, oneness). Nothing in and of its own self has life, character, quality, nature, condition or amount to it or about it; nothing of its own self has color or fragrance, body or location. Nothing is an entity, a being or a thing, an activity, a cause or an effect. No person, thing or condition has power over another. All is God; therefore all existence—no matter what we may believe it is, or what name we may give to it—is God, and is full of the goodness of God, "within and without."

What prevents us from experiencing our whole and complete good this day? What hinders our healing? What prevents us from standing strong in truth, dismissing appearance, and evidencing the forms of good (God) this moment?

Why do we fall, time and again, under the spell of collective belief, mis-identity and false experience despite being aware that God is all? What is stopping us from standing upright and walking free this day? *Only continued belief prevents or delays us.*

As long as we continue to believe in the personal self with its mental mind, physical body and material world, we are living by belief instead of truth. It is not at all easy to break free of belief, to stop indulging in personal sense. However, the freedom of good—not only as the healing of any illness, disease, lack or limitation we may be experiencing today, but as the transformation of our entire lives—exists here and now, whole and complete, fully demonstrated and already manifested in and throughout our consciousness.

Is this not inspiration enough to begin to drop belief and turn to truth; inspiration enough to seek "the kingdom of God" instead of continuing to suffer the kingdom of belief?

Realize this: in the very place that seems, to belief, to be diseased, poor, unable or unsafe, actually right there health, wealth, harmony and safety exist. The problem, whatever its nature, is never what it seems to be, nor is it rooted in what seems to have caused it. All problems stem from the one root problem: the *belief of being different and separate from God.*

Only God is; only love, life, wholeness, harmony and abundance are. God exists as true being and formation, the one reality, visibility, tangibility, manifestation and demonstration. The only truth of life is God and that truth exists in perfect and real form in and as your consciousness. "I and the Father are one." God "and" consciousness "and" form are one, not different or separate.

This being true, the question arises, *how* do we evidence

the truth of life? How do we experience the healing of problems? We have to know the *how* of the God experience because we hear the promises of truth, we practice as best we can, yet our problems refuse to yield. We continue to find ourselves challenged by ill health or disease, lack or limitation, unhappiness or insecurity even though God is omnipresent.

NO LACK OF GOD

Realize that no lack or limitation exists in God. And because God is all, which includes all form, no form lacks its perfect good and completeness. Admittedly, much good *seems to be* lacking almost everywhere we look, but that which seems to be is not that which *is.* There is no lack of good anywhere in the world because there is no lack of God anywhere in the world. There is just a lack of God *awareness.* Awareness and experience are one; therefore a lack of God awareness has the *effect* of making form appear to lack good.

Because God is all, you, I, all beings and all things are God; and because God is the only, the only faculty is God. This minute your truthful faculties of awareness have and see a body and world filled with God—good, wholeness and harmony. No lack of God exists, and because God is all, no lack of God form exists, nor the faculty of its awareness.

You cannot gain more of God because you do not lack any of God, nor can you gain more God faculty. You and your faculties are full of God, and those faculties are, this minute, seeing and experiencing a mind, body and world full of God—none else, none less, none lacking or in need.

Because this is true, you and all beings have the "ability" to evidence as much of God, good, as experience needs this day, with "twelve baskets full" left over.

Do you believe this? Ah, there's the problem! The God experience exists beyond belief. Truth is true, but its tangible experience exists beyond belief, in a God state of awareness. You, I and all are one existence—God-existence. The only mind you have is God-mind; the only body, world and universe you have, including every person, place and thing in it, is God.

"You" and "I"—if we continue to exist in a personal, material state of belief—lock ourselves out of the spiritual experience. We must lift into and maintain ourselves in a God state of being where all of God (good) exists in perfect visibility and tangibility. In a God state of being, spiritual awareness happens *as us* and *for us;* the good of God becomes evident and real *as us* and *for us.*

We must maintain ourselves, minute by minute, in the spiritual state of being where God infuses our awareness and lives life *for us.* Only God awareness is aware of God being, body and world. Only when God itself is being our awareness does God being, body and world become evident; only when God itself is being our clarity does the image and likeness of God become clear as all we experience.

What is the "God state" of being? It is a conscious state of oneness, in and as which nothing of "us" or "our world" is left in us (in our awareness). Once we are in a state of oneness, a nothingness of personal self, realizing (even though dimly) that in spirit all is one, whole and perfect, we rest and *feel God happening* within and throughout us. This state of rest and feeling God happening *is itself* the good of God evidenced; *is itself* the good or "healing" made visible and tangible in experience.

As we are in a God or spiritual state of being we are safe and secure. We do not have to "do" anything to bring about health and wholeness any more than the sunbeam, resting as one with the sun, has to do anything to bring about light and heat. Oneness *is,* and does the "work" of making good evident, "healing" that which is sick, poor or discordant.

We are not required to make effort for our good in oneness; we only have to *be in* a conscious state of oneness, and then behold God "at work." "He performs that which I am given to do. . . . He perfects that which concerns me."

We do not have to "make" any aspect of experience one and whole; all is already one and whole. What we have to do is attain and maintain a conscious state of oneness, of God, and then *behold* God in action. We lift or transform our state of awareness (mind) to that of God, spirit, oneness alone. "Do not conform to the way of this world, but be ye transformed by the renewing of your mind." We lift our awareness from the belief in "this world" (humanity and materiality) to become a being of God, of spirit, of oneness. We lift our awareness; we become filled with, interested in, and devoted to God not man, spirit not matter, oneness not multiplicity.

In this state of being (our natural, truthful state) we do not have to make mental or physical effort to achieve good. Yes, we feel the impulse to get up and serve in some manner, to do something of value, to be creative and giving, to go with the flow of the talent or idea that springs up within and animates us—the feeling that surges within and spills over into and as our work, our everyday demeanor. But we are never required to *achieve* the spiritual impulse and surge, or the health, harmony, happiness, prosperity, safety or security of our experience. The truth of life is free and unconditional. It is the "gift of God," the actuality of the finished kingdom, of oneness, of a God state of being.

Studying books and classes, meditating on truth, seeking God in one way or another are the efforts we make to achieve just one goal—the attainment of a God or spiritual state of being, a state of conscious oneness. It is the God state of being which *is itself* the evidence of God. Studying and gaining intellectual knowledge *itself* does not make God evident. God is already evident; it is *our* material state of awareness that clouds the evidence of God. We could continue for a thousand years to seek God through study, meditation and even silence; yet no more of God would be evident than it is this day.

This becomes clear when we realize that we could seek the sun by attending classes about sunshine, meditating upon the sun, praying for sun, even sitting in silence waiting for the sun to come to us. None of that effort would give us the actual experience of sunshine. Our study and contemplation is necessary because it opens our awareness to what the sun is and where it exists. Once we have that knowledge we can go to where the sun is shining and *there* have as much sunshine as we want or need.

In the same way, our seeking God, our study and meditation open our awareness to what and to where God is. They lift us into a God state of awareness, and *there* we have as much of God (good) as we want or need.

Good in all its formation is free and unconditional once we are *being what it is*—a God state of being. It is the God state of being that enables us to experience ourselves, others, and all the things of the world "as [they are] in heaven." Once we have attained the God state of awareness we only have to bathe in and behold God taking place as all. Healing of any and every disease, discord or lack then takes care of itself.

Is this not similar to our experience of sunshine? The only way we can experience the sun is to go to where it is shining, and then bathe in it. *It* does the work; *it* perfects our experience of light and heat. We cannot do that work, and we are not expected to. Only the sun is light and heat and only the sun can give it to our experience. What we can and must do is take *ourselves* to where the sun is happening. It is no use sitting in the dark, studying the sun, contemplating the sun and seeking the experience of the sun, hoping that these alone will give it to us. We will not have it or its benefits until we take ourselves to where the sun is shining.

When we "take" (lift) our state of awareness from human and material to God, we discover that *there*, in a God state of being, God is fully happening as us. *There* God is happening as the entirety of your universe and mine, inclusive of every form and detail of it. As soon as we are there, all we have to do is rest, be still, be silent and receptive—as a sponge in the ocean, or a window in the sun—as God fills our senses.

Once you know the truth and have attained a God state of being, rest and freely receive the life and light of God. "Know the truth, and the truth will make you free." Know that I, the very I of you, your consciousness—the entire and all-inclusive experience of you—is God. God's universe, God's being, God's mind, God's body, God's abundance, God's relationship, God's oneness, God's safety and security, God's home, God's business. All is forever and perfectly intact, *governed by God,* and tangibly experienced in, as and "out of" the God state of being.

In a human, material state of being we have only what humanity and materiality offer. We are being (and have) the pairs of opposites—belief—and the ongoing battle between the opposing pairs. But in a God state of being we are and have all that God is and has. "Son, I am ever with you, and all that I have is yours."

"KNOW THAT I AM GOD"

What is *I*? *I* is God, consciousness, the infinity and omnipresence of divine existence *being all.* "Be still, and know that I am God." Everything of and throughout infinity is *I,* God, consciousness. God is all. All that you are and have—every person, body, form, organ, function, sound, color, fragrance, place and activity (despite its corporeal appearance)—is God, *I,* consciousness, one.

All is God in perfect order—whole and complete, still, peaceful, blissful. Nothing of existence is other than or different from God. The one and the only being, mind, body, world and universe *is* God, forever in perfect form. "I am the Lord, and besides me there is none else."

What clouds, hinders or delays us from experiencing the perfect order and unconditional good of all? What clouds, hinders or delays us from experiencing healing? What hinders us from experiencing all the health, wealth, love, wholeness and freedom of being that we can ever want or need, not only for ourselves, but to share with as many as are seeking these themselves—whether that be one person, one thousand or ten thousand? Why do we still feel unsafe or insecure? Why do we feel threatened by one or another worldly condition or circumstance?

We *hear* that all is God, all is spirit, all is *one,* but we have not yet caught the subtle principle of the God experience—that all is *one: one life, one being, one body, one universal form.* That which appears to be countless degrees of good and bad being, health, finances and world conditions (multiplicity) is actually *one* (God) seeming, to sense, to be many.

Only *one* is—this is the key to spiritual awakening. Only *one* mind exists. We do not each have our own, different mind. Only one mind exists, that mind being God.

Only *one* body exists. We do not each have our own body, separate and different from every other body, any more than we have our own minds separate and different from every other. Only God is, and God is *one.* All mind and body are the *one* mind-body that is God—indivisible, inseparable; of one nature and quality, *appearing*, to sense, to be many individual, "different" minds and bodies.

Only *one* form, character, quality, condition, presence, amount and activity exists, and that one is God or spirit or I or consciousness.

Only *one* place exists, and that is holy ground. It is the place of *conscious oneness.* The place or consciousness of oneness is not corporeal, physical, material, objective, geographical or even nameable. It is the state of *being consciously one* rather than consciously diverse. It is the state of spiritual rather than material consciousness, a God rather than human state of being, as which all that "we" know, think and do is abandoned for oneness. It is the state of realization and living as God-alone-existent-as-all. "My thoughts are not your thoughts, and my ways are not your ways."

It is the awakened state of being that realizes that what we have believed to be real is not, because only God is; therefore only God is real. And because God is *one,* reality is one with not even one "other" in it.

Oneness itself, the *conscious state of oneness,* is God, which is truth, the universe of good without opposite. The state of conscious oneness is itself the one mind, one body, one place, *the one infinite and omnipresent formation of all.* This state of being is the God or spiritual state of being. No other state of being can evidence God because no "other" state of being is of God. All "otherness" is belief, or mis-identity, not truth.

Like recognizes like; only a God state of being recognizes and experiences a God state of mind, body and world. No other state of being but that *of God, sees* God, and *has* God-form as real and practical experience.

God is one, and God is consciousness; therefore a conscious state of oneness *is* God-being, *is* spiritual being, *is* the presence of God as earth (form).

The "practice of the presence of God" is the practice of being a conscious state of oneness.

The mistake we make, the subtle misunderstanding we have lived with, is believing in God "and" humanity, God "and" matter, God "and" world, God "and" circumstance or condition. This belief is not oneness but twoness or multiplicity.

Once you have caught the truth of God (oneness) being the only and are living in a God (oneness) state of being, beholding God revealed as the form of every moment, there is no need for another spiritual book or class. You can give all your books away. We do not need books or classes once we have caught the subtle truth of oneness and are living it. Once we live in even a grain of true conscious oneness, all our objective needs are taken care of—plus twelve baskets full left over. Wherever we are, there good and fulfillment are. We ignore and dismiss appearance as the nothingness it is of itself. We live in and experience the consciousness of truth—the infinity and omnipresence of God, good. Consciousness and form are one, so we never lack the tangible and practical forms of good.

HEALING OF PERSON AND CONDITION

In spiritual consciousness no person, thing or condition requires healing. All good and perfect condition already *is.* When a person calls for healing, the *apparent* he, she or it (the claim) is ignored as being a false picture only. Even if a person is face to face with me, explaining and seeking help for the problem, both the person and the problem are disregarded, and the presence of God is felt—tangibly experienced—as the only person and condition. *That is why the person experiences healing.* That is why what appears as false or misinterpreted pictures of person and condition changes to reveal truthful, healthy and harmonious pictures.

If I believed people and the problems they are suffering to be real in and of their own selves, there would be no healing. If I believed humanity and materiality to be reality, and then attempted to access God to heal that which was ill or discordant, yet ignored that which was good and harmonious, it is I who would need to attend classes, rather than give them.

Let us bring clarity to that which is misunderstood about God, "us," and the God experience (the healing experience).

God is one. Nothing exists that is *not* God. "All things [are] made by him; and without him [is] not any thing made that [is] made."

All is one, *the one,* which is God—one itself, with no "other." Nothing of life—not one being, body, organ, function, thing, amount or condition—is different from or less than God. All is *one*—indivisible, inseparable, eternal, in perfect form and order.

One cannot be altered or made imperfect, made different or less than one eternally is. Belief cannot alter God; un-God-like thought or action cannot alter God. Mis-identity does not change God. Nothing can change God because God is the *only.* It would take not only "another" but a "greater" power to change God. God is eternally its own God-like identity, its own image and likeness and cannot be altered. God is eternally God, and God is *all;* therefore all is eternally God, immutably being God-like identity.

Bring your awareness to *one.* Realize that *all* is one, just one. *One* is what God *is,* what spirit *is,* what the incorporeal *is.* All being is the one being, God-being; all mind is the one mind, God-mind; all body is the one body, God-body.

All place and condition are that of *conscious oneness.* There is no "other" than God, one.

Belief may label and describe form in ten thousand different ways, but those "ten thousand" describe *corporeal* images—people, things and conditions existing in time and space, and of a certain apparent quality and nature.

Our corporeal state of being presents us with corporeal people, things and places. In a corporeal state, we can visit any corporeal place, as long as it is corporeally open to our visiting it. But does that corporeal place provide us with spiritual experience? No. Only a spiritual state of being provides us with a spiritual experience. Only a state of *conscious oneness* provides us with the experience of oneness—wholeness, limitlessness and harmony. Only in a *conscious state of oneness* do we have the harmony, peace and perfection of God throughout our experience.

In conscious oneness we perceive our body and our world as God, oneness. Little account is taken of appearance or physical feeling. Our attention is on oneness, not on what appears to be—not on the apparent multiplicity which presents itself as images and suggests itself as being real. Multiplicity is, to us, an innocent and impotent three-dimensional imagery, a background movie. Our attention, our senses, are stayed in and as oneness, "here within." Each him, her and it that presents itself to us is known as God, not a personal being, not materiality.

In conscious oneness, that of us which is true, is the "cause" of our life, love, abundance, harmony and fulfillment. We are the "inner" presence of fulfillment experienced "outwardly" as our world.

3

SPIRITUAL RELEASE

IT IS PROBABLY TRUE that every individual yearning for truth *intellectually* grasps the reality of oneness. We "get" it each time we read or hear a truth message, but then we promptly continue accepting appearance as being real.

We ourselves, and the people, places, things, conditions, amounts and activities in our day are to us if we live in a human state of mind, what they *appear to be* rather than what they are: God or oneness. We continue to believe in and live by the personal, human self, the physical body and the material world, all of which are subject to many powers and pairs of opposites. We believe in spirit "and" matter, us "and" them, this "and" that, here "and" there, more "and" less, the universe "and" God—everything *but* oneness!

Then we wonder why our problems fail to yield, why we are stuck in humanity and materiality and their limits and struggles, what blocks truth from our experience. We reach for another book or attend another class searching for the answer. We believe it is *we* who do not yet have sufficient spiritual ability to experience our health, prosperity, harmony and wholeness so we get busy trying to gain what we believe we do not have. We are stuck in a seemingly endless cycle of belief trying to find freedom.

We have *personalized* ourselves and our experience. We have a *personal* body, with which we are either satisfied or dissatisfied. We are satisfied when the body is healthy, fit and strong, and because we're satisfied we do not seek truth. But when the body is sick, injured or old, we are dissatisfied and fearful, and we quickly get busy seeking healing, health and wholeness.

We believe we have *personal* dollars and personal means of making them. We intellectually know the truth of oneness (one substance, one form, one amount)—yet we continue to name and desire dollars and improved ways of making them. We continue to judge prices, respond to bargains, and make buying decisions based on price tags.

We intellectually understand that God, spirit, oneness is love, yet we continue to seek love from the outside world. We still expect cooperation from *human* relationships—from our employer or employees, our colleagues, from friends and neighbors. It is just as difficult to stop looking at humanity for love as it is to stop looking at dollars for wealth or the body for health. But we have to stop seeking "outer" love if we want true love, companionship and cooperation. We cannot continue to have God as love *and* look for love in or from human relationships.

We understand God as all, yet believe we own or rent a material home, in a structural neighborhood, populated with human beings, all with their own character and nature—some nice, some less nice; some quiet and considerate, some noisy and inconsiderate.

RELEASE APPEARANCE

If we are ready to lift out of the dark and limited belief in God "and," into the light and freedom of truth, and experience the real health, wealth, love, harmony and fulfillment of being that are our inherent truth; if we are ready to free ourselves from the prison of belief instead of remaining in a dream state, wondering why we do not experience the freedom of God-being; if we are now truly ready to walk into the light of God and have God or spirit fill our experience with *its* infinite, omnipresent and unconditional good, then we have to lift ourselves into a conscious state of oneness.

Let us now and forever lose the personal sense of *both* self *and* truth. The moment you realize and live as oneness, every aspect and condition of your life is released and is quickly free and boundless. "Whoever discovers the interpretation of these sayings will not taste death." (*The Gospel of Thomas.*) If you have "ears to hear" and "eyes to see" you will understand the truth given in these pages and walk free.

Your ears will hear and your eyes will see *God as all.* Your freedom and purpose of being flourish. The moment you find your way out of the dark and hardship of belief into truth, you never again believe what appearance suggests is real. The moment you lift yourself into a state of *conscious oneness,* then *rest receptively* in the love, peace, stillness and fulfillment of God-as-all, God "takes over."

God governs and reveals the harmony and wholeness of every detail of our lives *for us.* "He performs the thing that is appointed for me. . . . The Lord will perfect that which concerns me."

The presence and impulse of spirit so fills you and flows from you, that you find yourself thinking spiritually, acting spiritually and beholding the kingdom of God visibly and tangibly wherever you are. You find yourself full of oneness, living, moving and having your being in and as the kingdom of oneness, having an infinity of oneness ever at hand. Health, harmony and abundance fill your experience; sickness, disharmony and lack dissolve in your presence. Love, peace, success and security fill your experience as you live in your natural state of oneness.

This point of attaining conscious oneness, and truly living as and by oneness, is the "tipping point" of spiritual awakening. We "tip over" from belief into truth. From then on we live freely, effortlessly, harmoniously and purposefully. We have attained spiritual realization, spiritual identity, and we live by God instead of by personal sense.

ATTAINING THE TIPPING POINT

To attain the tipping point, attain the realization that all appearance in and of its own self is nothing more than *mental concept* or *imagery.*

That which appears to be real is nothing more than belief about that which *is* real: God, spirit and truth; oneness.

If we believe how he, she or it *appears to be,* we experience nothing but that belief. We cannot experience more or less than the belief we are *being.* We are imprisoned by our own state of belief.

Day by day, we are presented with many apparently good and bad conditions, but as long as we realize that everything that presents itself to us, both the good and the bad, is nothing more than concept or image, and that all actually is the *one presence of God,* then we are able to remain detached from belief and free in spirit.

Everything of appearance, in and of its own self, is nothing more than imagery, like images in a mirror. All appearance, of itself, is "mirror" imagery, with no substance, no life, no power, no form of its own.

Images are not entities but just pictures or reflections. They have no life, body, quality, character, condition or ability of their own; they are without law or principle; they are unable to sustain or maintain themselves in our experience. Belief supports and sustains them in our experience, but belief can operate in us only for as long as we are believers. Just as we have to stand in front of the mirror to have and sustain a mirror image, so we have to continue to believe in order to have and sustain the pairs of opposites—good battling with bad in experience. The moment we walk away from belief, the pairs of opposites lose their power and effect in our experience as quickly as mirror images vanish when we step away from the mirror.

UNDERSTANDING IMAGERY

The image or concept of any person, thing or place is also never "only" what it appears to be. Nothing is isolated and separate. All is one, and the *whole* of one. No person is "only" a person, no object is "only" an object, no place is "only" a place, no activity is "only" an activity, no amount is "only" an amount.

All is, and contains the *whole* of God, the *whole* of one, the *whole* of infinity and omnipresence.

Nothing is fixed or contained as belief suggests it is; nothing is "merely" what it presents itself as being. You awaken to this the moment you realize that all is God—infinity and omnipresence, incapable of being made finite and local.

The self and its faculties of awareness are that of God, of infinity and omnipresence. Therefore, what of you, or your experience, is fixed or contained?

You are and embody the entirety of being. The 7.3 billion people who populate our awareness (earth) at this time are all the *one being* we each are and each embody. In fact, the one being is infinitely greater than "only" 7.3 billion. God is infinite; therefore being is infinite. The whole of God is embodied in and as you, me, and all; therefore the *infinity* of being is what you are, and is embodied in and as you, me and all.

You are the whole of being, the one being, not a finite, personal, separate or different being.

"Son, you are ever with me, and all that I have [and am] is yours. . . . I and the Father are one." We intellectually grasp these truths, yet still believe that we exist separate and personally different from 7.3 billion others. We intellectually grasp that "you are ever with me, and all that I have is yours," yet we continue to believe that dollars are our supply, and are separate and different from our very being, and hard to get.

"Be still, and know that I am God." Somehow the intellect has taken "I am God" to mean the "truth" of I buried deep within, but not the reality and practicality of I and its everyday experience. We hear that "I am the Lord, and besides me there is none else," yet wonder how our healing, harmony and fulfillment will come about. We wonder how we can bring the health, wholeness and peace, the love and freedom of God we read and hear about into our human bodies and material worlds, and then get busy reading books and attending classes to find out.

There are plenty of teachings telling you "how to achieve it" that have nothing to do with truth *itself.* Truth itself is already whole and complete, and does not need a "method of demonstration" or of "manifestation." God *is,* and God's *truth is.* God is all; therefore God's truth is all. God is whole and complete, already fully manifested and demonstrated. We cannot *make* it so, nor are we required to. God *is.*

Realize that *all* of experience—the good and the bad—is *belief*-imagery. Reality is God, and because God is all, the only thing that presents itself to you is God—unconditional good. The *whole* of life—all the life that has been, is, and will be evident on earth and infinitely beyond—exists in and as you, *is* the life you are and have. None of life exists outside of you; none of life is different from the life you are and have.

Life is infinite, omnipresent and eternal. Realizing this, can you believe you have only a limited amount of life? Can you believe you live for only a few decades, at most, and then die?

All the life in existence is the life you, I and all are and have because "Son, {daughter], you are ever with me, and all that I have is yours. . . . I am that I am. . . . I am the only, and besides me there is none else."

Without you, God does not exist; without the blade of grass and without the color green of the grass God does not exist. Can you believe that? If you do not, or cannot, you have not yet realized that God is all, and God is omnipresence. Omnipresence cannot lack any particular element of itself. Either the whole of omnipresence exists, or omnipresence does not exist at all.

God, omnipresence, is *one,* whole and complete. God cannot be divided, separated into parts, made incomplete, made into two, or into a multitude. "All that I have is yours [is you, is me, is all of life and every form of life]." That "all" is omnipresence—forever whole, indivisible, inseparable, one. The whole of God *is* what you are and have. It is what the table I am working on is, what the candle on the table is, what the flowers by the window are, and what the window itself is. The whole of God is what every object, place, condition, color, fragrance, sound and activity *is,* and what all the thin air among everything *is.* If all of this did not exist, God would not exist because God *is all of this.*

If water did not exist, wet would not exist. The "two" are one and the same entity and cannot be separated. It is impossible to have water without wet or wet without water. Water *is* wet, and wet *is* water. We are not surprised at this truth, yet when we consider that God would not exist if even one of us did not (or even one object, color or fragrance did not) and that we exist as the entirety of God, some find it hard to believe, even sacrilegious.

GOD IS ALL

God is *all,* and God is *one,* inseparable and indivisible. We find this hard to accept only as long as we continue to believe that we and our world and all it contains are *different* from and *separate* from God. This belief is as untrue as the belief that water and wet are different and separate. "I and the Father are one," not two, not different, not separate. You and God, I and God, all and God *are one and here now.*

All is one; all is the state, or *es*tate of God (one)—the substance and presence; the perfect, whole and complete form of oneness, omnipresent as all.

Oneness is the one truth, yet how many times do we make, in belief, something "else" from one? How many of our fifty to seventy thousand daily thoughts are about something "other" than one or oneness? We believe in and think about "our" mind, "our" body, "our" health or ill health, "our" fulfillment or defeat, "our" happiness or unhappiness.

Being a happy human has made, in belief, something "other" out of God, and being an *un*happy human has made an opposite "other" out of God. As soon as we have "otherness" we have no God, nor can we find God to heal or fulfill our "otherness." We are living as a prodigal, different and separate *in belief* (never in reality) from that which we and our world actually are. Yet, even as we live as far away in belief from God as we can get, God is right here, perfectly real, practical and fully available to our experience. To have our good, we need only "turn back" from our prodigal belief, head home to "the Father's house" (God consciousness), and live as and by God, oneness, instead of as and by "otherness."

Making a dollar out of oneness instantaneously separates our sense from the infinity of wealth and prosperity we are and have, and which is as free as the air to our daily experience.

Believing we have human relationships instantaneously separates our sense from the one true relationship, which is that of God, oneness—love without opposite.

Believing our food to be different from the one food that is God, instantaneously separates our sense of experience from the one food, the one nutrition, the one value, taste and satisfaction of God as food. In that separated sense, we cannot taste or receive a fraction of the true nutrition contained in the food we eat. Even the simplest meal tastes like heaven and provides full and perfect nutrition if we know that it *is* heaven—oneness. If we do not know it, and we separate it by believing it to be "just a simple meal," we lose its heavenly value; we lose its true flavor, nutrition and fulfillment.

If we believe our minds and bodies to be different from God, spirit, oneness, we instantaneously separate our experience of the mind and body from oneness, from the heavenly form and vitality they truly are.

It is this sense of difference and separation from God

that leaves us unable to dismiss and walk through disease or accident, lack or limitation, injustice or immorality, poverty or starvation, into wholeness and harmony, and share it with all in our vicinity. Painful experiences, indeed, appear to be very real, and appear to have very real consequences at their own level, but they are *not* real in truth.

We have been unable to ignore belief in the reality of such experiences. We have believed we have to do battle with and overcome the "bad" of life in an attempt to live the "good" life. Lost in this pairs-of-opposites belief, we continue to suffer and battle with the bad; attempt to heal the ill, diseased and injured; provide charitable supplies and protection for the suffering, love and comfort for the brokenhearted. Much of this human effort is good and certainly helpful at its own level. But it misses the great truth and freedom of life, which is God, the one and only true existence.

The Master explains the secret in the parable of the wheat and the tares.

> Let both the wheat and the tares grow [exist] together until the harvest; and at the harvest season [at the moment of spiritual fulfillment or fulfilled realization]. . . pick out first the tares, and bind them into bundles to be burned [dismiss and throw out all belief about there being any existence other than God itself]; but gather the wheat into barns [rest with the fulfillment of God as all].

The "tares" have no truth to them. Only God is true. God *is* the only truth and reality of experience. Truth exists in all its perfect form right at the place we believe a problem exists (and at all places). The appearance of either good or bad is not what it seems to be, but is God.

The moment we bring ourselves into a state of conscious oneness we become empty of belief. Oneness cannot exist hand in hand with belief. Either we are full of oneness or full of belief (multiplicity). We cannot be *one* "and" multiplicity. The very act of spiritualizing our awareness *is* the act of emptying ourselves of belief.

By filling our awareness with God or oneness, no room remains for belief. In a state of true conscious oneness we easily stay detached from a world appearing to be filled with good and bad. We know that only God is, that good and bad are not reality, and we easily brush away the appearance of unreality. Even when good or bad comes nose-to-nose with us, claiming itself to be real, demanding our attention, we stay detached and free in spirit.

Conscious oneness is not easily fooled. Even if an appearance of disease suggests that it will destroy our body; if an appearance of lack or poverty suggests that it will wreck our finances or bankrupt our business; if an appearance of hate, injustice or inequality suggests that it will destroy our lives or the lives of our families or friends, we stay centered in oneness and detached from suggestion. We know that appearance is a lie, a false sense, a non-form and non-power of its own self, and that only truth is true. "Judge not by the appearance, but judge righteous judgment."

In a conscious state of oneness, we do not go to battle with appearance, but ignore it and *rest* receptively in God, feeling God's presence "taking place" so that the truth (health, harmony, abundance and freedom) which *is,* is able to become visible and tangible to our senses.

"In returning [to a conscious state of oneness], and in rest, ye shall be saved." Certainly, if an appearance is particularly intense or threatening, we may need to devote fifteen or thirty minutes, even an hour or more to reading or listening to truth and contemplating the reality of God before we reach a sufficient state of "release," stillness, and receptivity to feel the presence. Use the classes and books for this purpose. Meditate with them; contemplate their message, until you feel yourself "released," lifted and freer in spirit.

In this freer state we begin to have a real and palpable experience of oneness. We *feel* it; we experience it *happening;* we behold oneness taking place within us and throughout our consciousness, so much so that we are able to look "out" at our world, witness good or bad imagery, and ignore it. Oneness has become our predominant awareness. "One with God is a majority." We are so completely filled with oneness that the "rest" does not matter.

This is how we must feel in the world—strong in spirit, strong in oneness. Our strength of feeling is true conscious oneness. In that state nothing can hinder us, hold us back or make us fail. We have lifted above humanity and materiality which have many hindrances, delays and failures, into spirit which is and has only *good*—God, spirit and truth.

THE WAY OF HEALING

This degree of spiritual strength and conviction admittedly takes a real devotion to truth. We must fill ourselves with truth morning, noon and night, and if a problem presents itself to us, a problem that appears to be very real—a problem we feel threatened by or unable to quickly brush aside—we may need to read or listen to truth for many more hours before we feel released from the problem. Read this book or listen to a class, until you feel a spiritual response within you, an "Ah hah," a release; then stop and ponder that particular sentence or paragraph of truth for a few minutes; and then rest receptively with it in silence. Wait for the *feeling* of peace or warmth or love or light or a sense of greater release to well-up within. *This feeling or "happening" within* is *the wholeness and harmony of God (the healing) being experienced.*

However long it takes and by whatever means or combination of means you need this day—reading, listening, pondering, sitting in silence; and then reading a little more, listening a little more, pondering and sitting peacefully and receptively in more silence— *do this.* This is the way of healing. Keep going until you attain a state of spiritual peace which is greater than "you" and "your world"—greater than "the problem."

When you feel this state of greater spiritual peace, you have arrived at "the secret place of the most high." You have lifted above human and material sense, into spiritual sense; you have risen to *where God is* (conscious oneness), and to *where God is experienced happening as you,* your mind, body and world. As you have more of God happening in you than you have personal self, its world and its problem, your healing is taking place.

Conscious oneness is not only "where" God is but *is* "what" God is. When you are in a state of conscious oneness you *are one* with all the good that the world is and has because "I and the Father are one." God and form (the world, objective experience) are one; the world and God (truth) are one. All the good that the world is and has is yours as you remain in conscious oneness with God, feeling God happening within you and "out" as your world.

When you are in conscious oneness, you are *one with* and *as* God (truth) *as* the entirety of your experience. Every person, animal, plant, thing, amount, place, activity and condition—everything everywhere—*is now God and God-like.* As you stay in oneness, you are one with and as all.

When you are in a state of conscious oneness you are in God consciousness. We can describe it in many different ways—you have "arrived"; you are at the place where God is right there sitting with you, right there being the very you you are. God is right there being your mind, your awareness, your senses and your sensed body and world. Your mind is full of and aware of oneness. You are thinking of oneness; you are thinking about spiritual things rather than material things.

You "look out" at your world, and you realize that the people, places and activities you observe are not different and separate entities, but are God, spirit, oneness appearing as forms of experience. You observe a multiplicity of formation, but you know that there is only one—one being, one mind, one body, one formation.

You may observe one dozen or one hundred multifaceted forms this hour, each one seemingly different and separate—people, animals, objects, amounts, fragrances, colors, sounds and places. But you know that all is one. In this way, you stay in conscious oneness in the world. You remain consciously aware that the multiplicity of sense is *oneness* appearing to be "many," different and separate; *one* experienced as many facets, but always and only *one.*

MIND FORMS

Mind forms oneness into a multitudinous experience. Knowing this, we are able to "look out" and know that despite the multi-imagery we are presented with, all is one—God. All is *the one,* omnipresent, whole and perfect, peaceful and harmonious.

Sing the song of oneness, throughout your being. Constantly see, hear, taste, touch, smell and think oneness. Recognize all to be *the one* despite appearance.

In this state of oneness, rest receptively many times throughout the day and night, feeling God "happening." "Be still, and know that I am God." Bathe in that feeling as you would bathe in the sunshine. Let it fill you. Let it start living you while "you," like a bystander, observe it taking place. The "you" of you has become an observer. "You" are no longer living your life; God is living itself as you. "I live, yet not I, Christ [spirit, oneness] lives my life."

In letting God live itself as you, you become ever more released from that which appears to be good and bad. The sense of release and freedom in spirit, and of being filled with spirit, *is* the "healing"—the health, wealth, love, safety and security experienced. The release you feel is the release from the problem.

Daily lift into and maintain your awareness of one and let oneness live you. You will quickly become predominantly aware of *oneness*—God, spirit—being the only truth of mind, body and world. Your spiritual presence quickly becomes the influence, the cause, the very being *and form* of truth to and for your experience.

4

ONE

IT IS A STRANGE THING that as we seek God for corporeal good, we cannot find it, but as we seek God for God alone, we find God everywhere as corporeal good.

The reason is that God is *one.* If we bring even one additional idea or name to one, if we add even one belief, then we have *two,* which is not one. *One* cannot be two; one can only be one, and is only *evident* in a *conscious state of oneness.*

Two can never be one. When we bring even a single belief to one, we lose God altogether. We may believe we have God "and"—God "and" ourselves, our minds, our bodies, our loved ones; our finances, businesses, homes, neighborhoods, our worlds. But if we believe in God "and," we are fooling ourselves. Neither we nor a single place or condition in our universe contains God "and" because "God and" is impossible. What we have are two beliefs (two concepts), neither of which is God itself (and cannot be), even though we may *believe* one of them is God or that God is somewhere "in" our believed self or universe.

"GOD AND" IS NO GOD AT ALL

As soon as we introduce an "and" to our experience we have no God at all. God does not and cannot exist alongside an "and." God is not buried deeply within a believed personal self and universe. God is not the "higher self" and we the "lower self." God is *one,* God is omnipresence. God is the only. In all of existence there is no "and," no belief; there is just God, just one, just spirit and truth. "I am the Lord, and besides me there is none other."

God is *one . . . one . . . one.* Bring oneness up into your awareness. God is one . . . one . . . one. And because God is all, all is one.

A LENS OF VARIETY

When *one* shines through a lens of variety, one is observed as variety. If the lens contains ten different images, *one* is observed as ten different forms; if the lens contains ten thousand different images, *one* is observed as ten thousand different forms—as ten thousand different beings, objects, shapes, colors, scents, sizes, weights, amounts, places, conditions and circumstances.

One has not metamorphosed into many but is *experienced* as many. One is forever one and cannot be separated or divided into parts.

One is omnipresent. The whole is present and intact no matter how it appears to be.

God is *omnipresent one.* It is impossible for omnipresence to be divided and separated into pieces or portions; made into even two. One, which is omnipresence, forever remains one and omnipresent. Nothing in the infinitude can make one into two or into multiplicity. Nothing can be added to one; nothing can be taken from one.

One *is;* that is all there is to it. The multiplicity that seems to exist as our universe is *one*—God—simply experienced in an infinite variety of form, activity, thing, amount, condition and place. The multitudinous race of people and universe of things are not what they seem to be, but are *the one* which is God.

All of existence, God, is one—infinite, omnipresent, omniscient and omnipotent. Each being and "part" of existence are not separate entities "within" the universe, but are each the infinity, omnipresence, omniscience and omnipotence of *one. All appears to be* finite, local, separate and a "part" of the universe but is actually the one and the whole.

All, despite appearance, is THE ONE*—*THE *infinity,* THE *omnipresence,* THE *omniscience and* THE *omnipotence that is God.*

One APPEARS TO BE *many, but never actually is, and never can be, many.*

One forever remains one, whole, indivisible, inseparable, unalterable and incorruptible.

Each being, mind, body, organ, function, object, amount, place, condition and activity is not what it seems to be but is the WHOLE *and* FULL EMBODIMENT *of God.*

God, therefore *all,* cannot be incomplete, separated, divided, limited, finite, in lack, isolated or alone. One is the one, omnipresent, self-complete, all-as-all, all-in-all and all-of-all.

How can *one,* being inseparable and indivisible all, lack any of its wholeness and completeness, or be limited in any way? How can *one,* being unalterably infinite and omnipresent "also be" finite and local? It cannot. The *one* that God is *is* the *all* that self-body-universe is.

The belief in disease, lack and limitation; of isolation, of aloneness, of separateness, of a divided experience consisting of good and bad, and believed to need God for its healing is unfounded in truth. All belief is unfounded. *Only God is; only one is.*

Each and every person and thing is the *whole* of one. God *is the one, the* infinitude, *the* omnipresence, *the* omniscience and *the* omnipotence of all. You are that one, that allness; I am that one, that allness; all is that one, that allness.

One cannot be or consist of anything other, different or less. Each being and thing is the whole and finished kingdom of God; each being and thing is the finished kingdom of one—oneness itself.

Look "out" into your consciousness—into the room you are sitting in. Realize that God is and fills all space, and is itself all formation observed in all space.

God is all you experience, despite the way any he, she or it appears to be or is believed to be.

God is and fills all space; God is itself all the form I observe—whether human, animal, object, color, fragrance, place or activity.

One is the universe of being. One is consciousness and all "in" consciousness. No matter how near or far a person or thing seems to be, it is right here, as the oneness of you. *One* is the entirety of you, the entirety of your experience. One is sensed as a multitude of "animate" and "inanimate" form (mind-body-thing-world-universe), but all is the one, which is God.

Even though appearance testifies to there being many, there are not many; there is not an actual multiple of people, things, places, amounts and conditions. All is one—all is God. All "in" the universe is and has the quality, the nature, the character, the presence and the power of God. Nothing else, nothing different exists. *Only God is, only one is.*

Realize that your entire universe of awareness is God—*the one*—even though it appears to be a multitude. Multiplicity does not exist in one, but simply *appears to be.*

~

All is one, *the one.* The entire consciousness of you is God and full of God—one, just one. That *one* is not human, not physical, not material, but spirit; not temporal but eternal; not variable but invariable; not conditional but unconditional.

The *whole* of God (life, love and harmony; spirit and truth) is forever and unconditionally present and *being* all that you are and experience. You are spirit and truth; I am spirit and truth; all is spirit and truth.

*I am spiritual being, with spiritual mind and spiritual body, experiencing the spiritual universe. And because spirit is one—*THE *one—all that I am and have is one, infinity and omnipresence, wholeness and completeness.*

The kingdom of spirit (which is the only kingdom; the only being, form and experience) is forever in divine order, whole, complete, perfect. How important this is to know: God is forever in perfect order. Not one form or aspect of experience; not one thought, thing, place, activity or condition is out of order, incomplete, separate and isolated from the whole of good. All is one and inseparable; nothing lacks good, its fulfillment of being, form and function.

Nothing exists in a state of "otherness." Nothing *can.* All is the infinity and omnipresence of one which is unalterable.

One, which is itself infinity and omnipresence cannot be made finite or local; cannot be made to lack or to be limited; to be incomplete or dysfunctional; to be discordant in any way.

One cannot find itself in a position of struggle, of having to battle a disharmonious condition, to survive disorder.

One cannot find itself devoid of love, safety or security; happiness, joy or purpose; freedom and fulfillment of being.

One IS ITSELF the whole of God, the whole of life, the whole of love, the whole of infinity and omnipresence; the whole of God-presence and -formation.

One IS, God IS.

But it is only as *we,* by at least a discernable degree of continuity, bring *ourselves* into and maintain a *conscious state of oneness* that we find all these truths and promises becoming real and practical.

In *conscious oneness* we find our true and fulfilling life, the life that has seemingly been hidden from us, unobtainable, impractical and too good to hope for or to trust, while "we" have been left to do battle with ill health, lack and limitation. None of these struggles have anything to do with God or truth, but we have lived "outside of" truth in a conscious state of twoness, otherness and difference rather than of *oneness and wholeness.* We have lived in a state of believed multiplicity, of not only God "and" another, but God and a multitude of others. We have fallen foul of a multitude of beliefs and because belief and experience are one, our experience has been filled with legions of belief-forms—the forms of both good *and* bad.

Hear it. Because God is *one* and none other, and because God is consciousness, it is in conscious oneness that we find and *have* the life or healing that has so far eluded us. All the life, health and healing we can ever need or want is right here where we are, fully manifested and already demonstrated. All that God is is visible and tangible in the most real and practical way *in and as oneness.*

There is no such thing as unreal or impractical God, but we must realize that God is *one;* and because God is consciousness, it is a *conscious state of oneness* that evidences the reality and practicality that God is.

If healed and healthier, more vital life is what we need, we have only to realize that our true body is in perfect form and function, fully manifested and demonstrated here and now. Our perfectly healthy body is forever present, unchanging; tangible and real and evidently so in our *conscious state of oneness.*

Life *is,* and the is that life is is omnipresent; and because there is no such thing as "unformed" or "uncreated" life, we only have to *find* life and its perfectly healthy body-form in our awareness. Once we have found it, we *have* it as our body experience.

If we lose our car keys we do not think in terms of having to create them. We know that they are already created. We do not believe that we have to demonstrate them. We know that they are already demonstrated. We also do not believe that we have to heal them. They were never sick. We only have to *find* that which is forever whole, complete, visible, tangible, real and practical, which we have temporarily lost sight of.

In the same way, we have temporarily lost our sense of life, health and vitality, yet it is right here where we are. We have only to *find* it.

Life, which is self-inclusive and all-inclusive embodiment (just as water is self-inclusively and all-inclusively wet), is one. And because life is consciousness, the life or healing experience is *conscious oneness experienced.*

Nothing of life inclusive of its infinite formation is hidden when we realize what life is, where it is, and how it is found—where it is to be experienced, where the reality of life is freely available as our one and actual practical reality; what the visibility and tangibility of life is, and how it is seen and "owned."

ONENESS

That life, that reality (the only life and reality) is *oneness.* Lift yourself into a conscious state of oneness and then simply sit still and receptive. Let oneness live you. You will quickly have your tangible health or healing, your vitality and strength, your whole, true and real life.

Life *is itself* oneness; oneness *is itself* life—the life of the very body you experience. The healing and continued health of the body is *oneness experienced.* This body is the one body, the body of *oneness,* which is God or spirit.

The spiritual body is never sick, decrepit or dead, but belief makes it *appear to be.* Belief makes our physical *sense* of body appear to exist as a state of opposites: healthy, youthful and vital versus sick, diseased or depleted. But belief is not reality and cannot affect reality. The real body remains in perfect spiritual form and function, entirely unaffected by the thousands of beliefs held about it. The real body is *one—spirit—*and that spiritual body exists eternally in all its glory, vitality, beauty and purpose here and now, in and as oneness, and is ever available to real and practical experience.

Experience your real body now. It is waiting to be found. Go to it, pick it up in awareness, and *let it be experienced* by letting God experience it *for you.*

As you do, you will begin to realize that if you are (or any person is) suffering disease, injury or decrepitude, the real body can be found, picked up, and "within three days" brought forth. The "three days" are the length of time it takes us to realize, feel and sit silently experiencing the spiritual body coming forth as spiritual awareness. In a sufficient state of spiritual identity and silence this is achieved.

When it is known *what* the body is and *where* it is to be found, where it is picked up and lived in its whole and vital state, any individual is readily able to experience the true body. When the true body is lived, the sense of body not only heals, and heals quickly if not spontaneously, but it is from then onwards immune to illness, disease, accident, decrepitude and death.

MIND FILLED WITH GOD

In conscious oneness, we find our mind full of God and all the spiritual good and good form that God is. The mind of God is the one mind, the mind of oneness. Mind is not many, not 7.3 billion different minds in as many different people. God is one, and because God is all, mind is one; and because mind is form, form is one.

Because God is spirit, mind is spirit and spiritual. When we want to find that mind—when we have at last decided to give up the belief-mind and the struggle with its false forms—and find truth, we go to oneness and discover that the one mind is right here, ever available for us to take up.

The one mind is your mind. It exists in its fullness, ready to be picked up in awareness, adopted, and *rested in.* It is full of the good and clarity of God as every detail of you; it is and contains every person, form and amount of God, which is your fulfillment of being. You are ready to pick it up and are seeking it aright when you seek *oneness.*

The oneness of mind is the God, Christ or Buddha mind. To "have" it, we must put aside *our sense* of mind and let the one mind take over; let the one mind fill our sense with *itself, its* formation and *its* experience.

Is there a single thing to be concerned about or to battle with when it is realized that our minds, bodies and world are oneness—infinity, omnipresence, omniscience, omnipotence and eternity? Oneness is *where* and *what* our mind-body-world is. When we know that oneness is spirit not matter, infinity not finiteness, omnipresence not locality, eternity not temporality, what is there to be concerned about?

When we know this truth, do we have to struggle with our believed sense of mind, body or world? Do we have to sustain the body's health and youthfulness with pills, potions or surgical procedures? Once we realize that God is all and is eternal life, health, beauty and youthfulness, and that God is *oneness,* all we need do is lift into and remain in a conscious state of oneness, and let oneness experience itself as the mind, body and world we used to call "us" and "ours."

The experience of oneness is free and unconditional. If we need healing we are healed; if we need a greater sense of life, vitality, strength and purpose we find ourselves filled with these. The minute we get to oneness, *there* the good and harmony of life *is.* It exists there for our free and unconditional experience.

Go to oneness and experience your mind, body and

world of truth. Nothing is hindering you. "Who did hinder you that ye should not obey the truth? . . . Arise, take up thy bed, and walk."

ABUNDANCE

In conscious oneness we find our infinity of form, including the infinity of the form we call "money."

In conscious oneness, good is not only limitless but omnipresent. Oneness *is itself* the infinity and omnipresence of all form. Money is just one of the boundless varieties of form we experience and is no different from or harder to evidence than any other.

If it appears that you are lacking a sufficiency of money, opportunity, customers, clients, patients, students, friends, colleagues or companions realize the non-truth of such suggestions. Lack does not exist; limitation does not exist; insufficiency does not exist; need or want does not exist. Only God exists, and God is infinite and omnipresent at every place and as all being and form.

Realize this truth. Stop struggling with belief and its false imagery. Realize that the only reason you or I will experience a lack of any form, including money, success, prosperity and freedom of expression is because we have been living with belief instead of God. We have had God "and"; we have had two. Most likely we have had many more than just two. The moment we have even God "and," we have no God. We have two *beliefs about* God, but no actual God.

But when we know that God is one and bring ourselves into a conscious state of oneness, realizing that oneness *is* infinity itself, and not only infinity but the omnipresence, omniscience and omnipotence of all; when we realize that by living in the conscious experience of oneness happening, all the forms of our experience evidence the harmony of oneness, then all we have to do is rest in oneness and let oneness repair our experience.

We then begin to notice our experience filling with the infinity and omnipresence of oneness. It does not matter what name or description we give to one or a multitude of forms. Our experience fills full of the oneness we are *living*, that we are now *being*, that we know all form, all experience, actually *is* and is full *of.*

"The earth is full of the goodness of God." The earth (including everything everywhere in it and of it) is not the multiplicity of different and separate beings, things, conditions; causes and effects; time and space that it appears to be, but is one and omnipresent. The whole of infinity is one. The macro of apparent multiplicity is actually the micro of one.

Because mind is form, and mind is infinite in idea and expanse, mind is observed or experienced as an infinite variety of formation, a magnificent expanse of three-dimensional and five-sensed form. But variety, idea or form are unchanged oneness. One forever is and remains one—the one presence, one quality, one nature and one condition, "inside" and "out"; nothing other, different or less.

LOVE

In conscious oneness we find our love and relationship—our one most intimate, and that of family, friend, neighbor or colleague.

Our conscious oneness is our oneness as and with all being, all condition, all activity, all expression. As we know oneness to be all, despite appearance, despite suggestion, despite belief, then of course as we live as oneness (or more accurately, as oneness lives us, as oneness instead of belief is being our experience), oneness is one *as* all being, all relationship.

There is no separation, no division. Oneness is all; therefore all is *the* one, *the* infinitude, *the* omnipresence, *the* omniscience, *the* omnipotence of one. Conscious oneness *is itself* our oneness as and with all relationship.

The first effort we have to make is to bring ourselves to oneness. We have to bring ourselves home, to our truth. We have to drop the variety and multiplicity of experience, the good versus bad, realizing that it *of its own self* is nothing. We have to lift into oneness by contemplating oneness, God, infinity, omnipresence, spirit, the incorporeal one presence, one being, one form. Once we are home in oneness, we rest and *let* oneness itself, God itself, the whole universal consciousness itself *be revealed* as loving and fulfilling relationship.

ALL IS

Nothing has to *become* whole and complete; nothing has to evolve. Nothing, not even God, has to *produce* good, harmony, health, abundance, love or peace in the body or the world. God, which is all, already *is* one.

One is whole*ness* and complete*ness*—miracles of experience that we could not even begin to describe.

This is what one is, this is what *is* is, this is what the you of you *is,* the I of you *is;* what mind *is,* body *is,* being *is,* amount *is;* this is what all *is.*

We forever are and experience oneness even though our experience seems to be a multiplicity, a world and universe of difference.

Existence is not a multiplicity or a variety. Existence is one because only one is. As we rest in *one,* we rest in *is.* We rest in the *is* of the finished kingdom. We do not attempt to use God or oneness. Do not attempt to have God fulfill "your" belief, "your" sense of need, "your" sense of being, and not only fulfill it but fulfill it by a certain date. Do not attempt to use God. You will fail. God cannot be used.

God *is;* therefore *nothing can be used.* God *is,* and God is all; therefore all *is.* Can you deeply and thoroughly hear that? *Nothing can be used.* Nothing can be used to achieve something else—to achieve gain, glory, result—because all already *is.*

God is that *all;* so do not try to use God. And do not try to use anything of the world because everything of the world *is* God. Simply rest in *is.*

All *is,* and if all *is,* all of experience *is.*

Think on these truths.

5

MIND AND BODY

IF GOD IS ALL, which God is, *mind is God.* Do not attempt to use the mind to achieve a result, to manipulate or create good, or to heal. Instead, realize that the mind *is,* and that *is* is already the whole of God, infinity and omniscience aware of its one form as all. Release the mind and let it be your faculty of spiritual awareness. When you do, it presents you with the glorious and united spiritual universe, populated with spiritual beings, things and conditions, in perfect order and about their divine purpose.

Body *is.* Do not attempt to use the body, and do not attempt to use the mind to heal the body. Do not even attempt to use spiritual awareness to heal the body. If you attempt it, God is unavailable to your experience; you do not have any of the spirit you believed could be used to heal the physical body.

You cannot use God or spirit to heal the physical body because the body is already God and in perfect spiritual order. The body is spirit, the one presence, form and function which is God. The body does not need anything from us except to be recognized for what it is, and to be left alone to *be* what it is: God, spirit and truth, divinely and eternally healthy, purposeful and free.

Leave the body alone and get into oneness. Realize that *oneness is the body.* The physical sense is not the truth of the body. Oneness is the truth of the body, its only truth, its only formation, organ and function.

Leave the body alone; leave the physical sense alone, and come to where the *real body* is. The real body is fully and eternally functional and purposeful. Come to where this body exists. Come to the truth of this very body by dropping the false sense of it. Come to oneness, rest in oneness, and let the spiritual body reveal itself as the sense of body.

Simply rest, and *feel* (experience) God happening as itself, as *one—the* one that *is* you, *is* all.

Feel God happening as your entire sense of, and practical, tangible experience of, the universe—of mind, body, and all.

Experience the spiritual you, body and universe, not the false, material sense of these.

SPIRIT NOT MATTER

Oneness is spirit, not matter. What is called "matter" is sense. *All* is spirit. Our corporeal or material sense of spirit, in and of its own self, is not erroneous. There is nothing erroneous about sense. Leave sense alone. Realize that the infinity of sense is one, the one which is spirit, not matter, physicality or mentality, but spirit. In this realization, rest and simply *behold* the miracle of God *being* all.

Rest realizing that God, therefore *all,* is already whole, complete, finished, and forever in perfect order. As we stop struggling, stop doing battle with that which seems to be real and instead rest in that which *is* real, we are flooded with spiritual light and peace. Our senses are filled with truth. Our minds and bodies are illumined and experienced as they truly are—healthy, vital spiritual form and function. Spiritual good fills our world. Spiritual reality is illumined and alive in us.

"I [oneness] have food the world knows not of." I, oneness, have form the world knows not of. I, oneness, have life the world knows not of. I, oneness, have abundance the world knows not of. I, oneness, have customers, clients, patients, students, friends, companions, colleagues that the world knows not of.

I, oneness, have love and relationship the world knows not of, and knows not how to experience, or how to find. I, oneness, have peace and harmony, stillness and silence the world knows not of, and knows not how to experience. I, oneness, am and have safety, security in all its ways and forms that the world knows not of.

I have spiritual awareness and spiritual experience the world knows not of. But that *I* that is and has all of this is *oneness. I* does not consist of two or more. We must not name people, things and conditions as if they were real of their own selves. All apparent beings and forms are *one* (God) appearing, to sense, to be many. We have to know that all is *the one,* and nothing but the one—one with not even two, not even one other. There is the secret, and the experience of the true good.

~

I have God manifestation and demonstration the world

knows not of and knows not how to experience. A conscious state of oneness is and has the fullness of God manifestation and demonstration—not *to* be, or *to* gain, or *to* manifest or demonstrate; but *I am* the demonstration, *I am* the manifestation, and that *I* that I am is a conscious state of *oneness.*

~

I am and have God visibility and tangibility the world knows not of. Nothing is hidden in the mind of God, the mind of one. Nothing is un-manifested or un-demonstrated in the mind of one, the mind of God; nothing is invisible or intangible in the mind of oneness.

Nothing has "yet" to be present in the mind of God. God *is,* and because God is one and all, *all* of God is already and forever present, unfolding in our awareness step by step, hour by hour, day by day as the harmony and wholeness of formation—all being, organ, function, place, amount and condition.

ONENESS *IS*

Oneness is. We are no longer of anything but oneness; we no longer live by anything but oneness. It is because of oneness *lived* that all is whole and complete.

When we have and we live by and out from oneness; when we know that the multiple variety of formation and experience is not what it appears to be, but is *the one;* and when we know that that one *is* wholeness and completeness, *is* the finished kingdom, *is* infinity, omnipresence, omniscience and omnipotence, how on earth can anything be incomplete? How on earth can anything lack or be limited? It cannot. How on earth can anything be or remain ill, diseased, injured or decrepit? It cannot. But we have to know that *one* is the *only,* and we have to then *be* a conscious state of oneness. We have to *let oneness itself live* everything we are and have. We have to let oneness *be* our experience *for us.*

"My peace I give unto you." My light I give unto you; my spiritual awareness, and the fullness of it, I give unto you. My spiritual vision, my visibility, my tangibility I give unto you. But you must come to where I am, and that is a conscious state of oneness.

My peace, my oneness I give unto you. Only come to where I am—oneness.

GOD IS NOT A SERVANT

God, being principle (one) does not and cannot serve us. God is not an employee to whom we give orders and from whom we expect results.

God is God alone. Do not attempt to "use" God, "use" oneness, "use" spirit." Do not attempt to use the peace you feel filling you for human good or worldly gain, to use oneness to gain a "thing." Do not seek God for your or the world's purpose. Simply rest in the presence of God, in the presence of one (of I), in the presence of *is.* Rest in the presence of the only time that exists, which is now, this second. Rest in and as oneness, nowness, isness.

All that God is and has is experienced in the presence and peace of oneness which constitute harmonious, abundant and fulfilled experience. "I go before you to make the crooked places straight. . . . In my Father's house are many mansions. . . . I go to prepare a place for you." *I* prepares mansions of good, mansions of awareness, mansions of tangible experience; mansions of mind, mansions of life, mansions of bodily health, vitality and eternity, mansions of abundance, mansions of love and happiness, mansions of purpose and freedom.

Rest and relax in *I. Feel I* happening in and as and throughout you as every detail of your universe.

God is the only reality and practicality; God is the *oneness* that *is* reality and practicality. God, oneness, *is* the mansion of experience. Conscious oneness *is* the mansion of being, mind, body, world and universe. Conscious oneness *is* truth experienced.

God is omnipotence. God itself, conscious oneness itself, is the one power and presence of all experience, the one power and presence of harmonious, peaceful and fulfilled life. Omnipotence is the one power, one presence, one form. You do not have to use a "personal" power; you do not have to think or act in a certain way to "create" life or healing or vitality.

You do not need to think or act in a certain way to create abundance, success, financial security, to create love and loving relationship, or harmony and peace between people, neighborhoods, businesses and nations. All of God creation already *is.* All of creation is the finished kingdom of God, which is omnipotence, omnipresence, omniscience, infinity and eternity.

Nothing exists that is not God. God is all, and because God is good alone, all is good. "God saw every thing that he had made, and, behold, it was very good." The all good that God is is all that you are and all that you experience. You are only required to rest, relax, and behold the miracle of God happening as and in and throughout you—your consciousness, your entirety.

Do not be concerned about anything of appearance, of form or condition, in and of its own self. God is greater than all because God *is* the one presence and power of all. The "all" that God is greater than is belief and its appearance-form.

No appearing form, condition or amount; nothing of mind, body, business, finance, relationship, neighborhood, nation or world *in and of its own self* has any reality to it, or operating in it, that can, for even one more hour, sustain itself in your experience.

None but God is. The multiplicity of experience and all form and power of it are nothing in and of their own selves. He, she or that which is least in the kingdom of God is greater than he, she or that which is most powerful in the world. "Greater is he that is in you than he that is in the world."

He that is in you, oneness that is your (and your world's) truth, is not only greater than any one thing in the world but is greater than the everything in the universe put together.

He that is least in the kingdom of God is greater than he or it that is most in the world—the most terrifying disease or injury, the most life-threatening, the most financially threatening lack, limitation, condition or problem, the most difficult of relationships, the most seemingly insecure and unsafe circumstance, the most threatening war, the most overwhelming natural disaster. No matter what the problem or threat to one's life, safety or security, it is as a drop of water to the might of the ocean.

Just as the least of the ocean is greater than the most of the drop of water, the least of conscious oneness is greater than the most in the world.

Even if the entire world were threatened by disease, financial ruin or war, it could not and would not affect you or me, even by our least amount of conscious oneness, because "He that is least in the kingdom of God is greater than he that is most in the world."

"My Father is greater than all." As we abide in "the Father"—in conscious oneness—we have, and are beholding the greatest presence and power of all, the power that dissolves all discordant, disharmonious, diseased, lacking and limited sense-form.

Conscious oneness reveals itself as the truth of form just as easily as the light of the sun dissolves the dark of night. Conscious oneness *is* the one power and presence of God, the almighty.

When we step into and abide in conscious oneness, in "the Father," we *have* all the harmony that God is, and we have it *now.*

I is, and *I is* now. *I is* the truth and reality of you and of all, and is present and visible this minute, but realize that *I* and *is* and *now* are oneness. Rest in oneness. Rest in the one truth and then *let* and *behold.*

Let and behold; never concoct and make effort for. Rest and behold the presence and form of God. Rest and behold the presence of *one* become clearly visible and tangible to and as and for you *as* the whole of experience.

Simply know—restfully, peacefully and confidently know—that no matter what your world of good and bad looks like, it is the fullness of God. "The earth is full of the goodness of God"—full of the awareness of God, the visible, tangible, manifested and demonstrated good of God, the oneness of God.

Never take thought for your good; never make effort for your good. Simply come to oneness, and then rest and behold the miracle of God happening as and *for you.*

Earthly power, condition or circumstance, thing or activity has no power in the presence of the *one* power—oneness itself. Oneness (stillness, silence, beholding God taking place within) is greater than all in the world.

Keep this in mind moment by moment. *Conscious oneness* is greater than all in the world and quickly proves itself to be so. Just come to oneness, rest in oneness, and behold oneness happening in you and through you as the harmony of experience. Then watch how quickly and naturally discord dissolves.

It does not matter whether your world seems to be so threatening that it will finish you by tomorrow, bankrupt you, ruin your relationship, take away your home or business, leave you destitute and without hope. It does not even matter if death seems imminent. Simply come to oneness, rest, and behold oneness acting and resolving everything for you. "I go before you to make the crooked places straight."

Do you see? *I* goes before you.

"Before you call I will answer." *I* go before you. *I* act for you. *I* am the activity of truth in, as, through, and *for* you that melts all discordant, diseased, untruthful, limited and lacking experience. It does not make a difference what appearance suggests is reality. "He that is least in the kingdom of God"—that is you and me, he and she who are the least able to lift and stay in conscious oneness, but are trying our best to—"is greater than he that is most in the world."

There is no need to attempt to "use" God to heal or save you or any condition that is threatening you. Never attempt to use God, use oneness, use peace for anything. The attempt to do so will cloud the evidence of your harmony as quickly as closing the blinds shuts out the sunlight. You need make no effort, even mental effort. Simply rest and behold the reality of the *I* of you, the oneness of you *being* the harmony of all in your life.

Rest and know that your entire consciousness, your all-inclusive experience of being, is God and is filled full of the presence and power, the perfect and abundant formation, of God. Know that God is unconditionally yours in real experience as you come to one, abide in one, and let one be everything of experience for you.

Let oneness live you. "I live, yet not I, Christ lives my life." God (Christ, Buddha, oneness) is and lives my life *for me.* The earth is visibly full of the goodness of God *when* we know that the earth is in fact God, and we continually let it, through our stillness and receptivity, our nothingness of self, reveal itself as our harmonious experience.

ONENESS IS FULL OF THE GOOD OF GOD

Oneness is full of the goodness of God. Go to one and experience the fullness of that good. It is yours freely and unconditionally.

Most importantly, as we know this one truth, as we continually go to oneness, as we maintain our conscious oneness as best we can, and as we rest and behold oneness *being itself as* our mind, body and world, then it is—and this is our purpose of being—that we not only experience "our" healing and harmony but are the influence of truth for every person, thing and condition that touches our consciousness. I exist and you exist so that the glory of God can be revealed, so that the truth of all be revealed. In and as oneness, truth is revealed. This is the most important reason for our awakening, for our living in truth.

We do not need to find a way of healing, prospering or bringing love, peace, purpose or fulfillment to ourselves. Good heavens, we already are and have the whole of God, the whole of life, love and infinity in the palms of our hands; and when we go to oneness and abide there, we very quickly discover that we do. We very quickly discover that all the promises of God are true, but they are not to endow a personal self with longevity, beauty, love and riches. Rather they are to lift, feed, comfort and reveal the truth of the world.

"I am the light [oneness] of the world," and when I know this truth and am letting oneness itself *be the light of truth for me,* then it is tangibly true that I am the light of the world, that I am the food, comfort and healing influence in and for the world.

I am the light that fills every person, place and condition, dispelling the fog of sense, awakening all to the clear-seeing of truth in all its infinity and omnipresence of good.

Truth is not about satisfying the personal self but about discovering and revealing the *one* that God is as all. When this greatest of all principles is discovered, and when our intention and effort are truly to evidence the universality and omnipresence of God, we find every category of life—both that of "ours" and that of "others"—equally filled with the treasures of good.

6

I AND EXISTENCE ARE ONE

LET US BECOME QUIET, take a deep breath of relaxation, and feel a receptivity within.

Know that you are open and receptive to the message of truth. As you read, realize that you do not have to make truth true. Truth is already true. All the truth you are reading about is already the truth of you.

All you have to do is lose the *belief* that your existence—every form and aspect of it—is different from that of God. In the awareness that all is God, rest and freely receive.

We do not have to struggle to attain God; we do not have to grasp for truth. If we struggle and grasp, truth seems to run from us. It's a strange thing. The more effort we make to "get" God the more of good seems elusive. But the moment we know that God already is, relax receptively, and *let truth fill our awareness* (which it quickly does as we let it), we discover that we've had it all this time.

Truth *is* already and eternally who we are, what we are, what our minds are, what our bodies are, what our entire universe is, and what it all consists of. All is already God, but because we have not believed it, because we have misidentified who we are, what we are, what we have, we have not tangibly had it.

We have struggled for God like a drowning person struggles for air, and we have discovered that God runs from us. But if we stop our struggle, stop doing battle with that which seems to be, and simply sit still, quietly receptive, we quickly discover that God is right here where we are.

God is right here *being* us and all. God, being the only, the one existence, is what we are and what we have—every form, place and condition of what we have. Be still, rest; be quiet, be confident. There is nothing to be insecure or fearful about. Be confident in God and simply allow the light of truth to permeate your senses, to overflow as your presence of being, your mind, body and universe and everyone and everything, every place and condition, every activity and amount in and of your universe.

A WORKING PRACTICE

How much we have longed to find "the secret place of the most high." What we would give to find it, to be able to rest in it, to be able to see ourselves and our universe out from the secret place of the most high.

"The secret place of the most high" is the secret place of oneness—the conscious state of oneness. Intellectual oneness does us very little good. But *conscious oneness,* which is our bringing our awareness into a conscious state of oneness (the recognition and *feeling* of *one* being all) is the "secret place," the secret state of God-being, or God-consciousness.

Let me give you a working practice—a working meditation (below). As you keep this up, it will quickly evidence the fruits and treasures of the kingdom of God throughout your life—good without opposite. It quickly transforms any discordant or diseased or lacking or insecure or unjust or seemingly hopeless experience, and reveals its harmony, peace and fulfillment. Follow this and use it as a practical way of meditation to lift into and remain in conscious oneness. "Thou wilt keep him in perfect peace whose mind is stayed on thee." Keeping awareness *stayed on God,* on one, *is* the "secret place," the secret state of being. It is the secret of the practice of oneness.

God is one, just one. All that you are and all that you experience—all that you see, hear, taste, touch and smell, all that you think and all that you think about; all of your universe and everything everywhere in it and of it (every person, thing, place and condition)—is, despite appearance, just one.

All is one, THE ONE *that is God and nothing else. God is not two, not "and" anything. God is one, and that one is spirit—incorporeality. God is not matter or corporeality, but spirit, incorporeality.*

"Ye are the temple of the living God." Your I, your consciousness, your all-inclusive being and universe (both your most "inner "and "outer" experience) is the temple of the living God, the temple of consciousness—the temple of the living oneness, the living spirit, the living awareness; the temple of the conscious God awareness.

Consciousness is your universe and consciousness is God. God is and fills your universe. God is the very life, form and function of your existence; God is your mind, your body, your world, your entire global experience and all the form that constitutes it.

God is all; God fills all. God is the very formation of all, the very everything everywhere of your consciousness from that which, to sense, exists right in front of you, behind you, to the left and right of you, up and down, from the deepest "inner" to the most distant "outer" form or thought.

God is it. This is the actuality of you which is called "the temple of the living God"—the entirety of your consciousness.

As we remain consciously aware of this truth, as we keep our mind stayed on God, we are in the secret place or state of conscious God awareness. As we stay in conscious God awareness we *have* all that God is and has. We *have* the infinite and omnipresent gift of God, the gift of the oneness of all.

We do not make effort, we do not struggle. We do not have to. We do not have to do battle with anything of sense, good or bad. *In conscious oneness,* we are and have the living temple of God, the living consciousness of God because we have brought *ourselves* (our awareness) to that secret place and, therefore, experience the treasures of God throughout our consciousness (our universe). Here, there and everywhere becomes evident as God, good. False experience dissipates and truth emerges.

Once we are in a conscious state of oneness we can relax. There is nothing to fear. We can rest and *behold* God in action because in a conscious state of oneness the whole of the kingdom of God is laid out before us. We do not create; we behold. We are not creators, but "servants"—as the sunbeam "serves" the sun and the wave "serves" the ocean.

God is creator, created and creation—all one. We are the

"children" of the creation. Children are not expected to create their lives. Children receive the gifts of the parents; and as the offspring of God, we receive the gifts of God so that our lives may be abundant. "I am come that you may have life, and have it more abundantly." This not only speaks to immediate life but the whole of life in all its forms and categories. We have all of life more abundantly as we stay in conscious oneness and behold the kingdom of "earth as it is in heaven" full of the gifts of God.

"Ye are the temple of the living God." The promise or principle of God is "I shall dwell in them, and walk in them; and I shall be their God, and they shall be my people"—people filled with the goodness of God, the oneness of God, the one gift of God which dissolves all that is un-God-like. In conscious oneness there is none other, nothing different, nothing less, nothing opposite.

"I WILL BE THEIR GOD"

"I will dwell in them, and walk in them, and I will be their God, and they shall be my people." In that case, for what do we need to take thought? What do we need to correct, make good? What do we need to transform, prosper, pacify, heal?

How can we continue believing that we are responsible for our fulfillment, our life, health, happiness, love and prosperity when we hear "Ye are the temple of the living God" and "I will be their God"? You are not what you have believed you are. You are the temple of the living God.

I will dwell in you, and walk in you, and I will be your God, and you will be my person. I will be your good, and you will be my person filled with good—the person of God, the person who has and experiences good without opposite.

"The earth is full of the goodness of God. . . . The earth is the Lord's and the fullness thereof," but until it is realized that God is *one,* and that *one* is all, such spiritual promise and assurance is of no avail to tangible experience. The promises of truth are impractical because we have not made God the *one* and the *only* in us and of us, and the *one* and the *only* of every aspect of our experience. We believe that we and our experience are different and separate from God—something other than or less than God, something other than oneness. Such belief is untrue. It is because it is untrue that we have been unable to evidence that which is true.

GOD IS ONE AND OMNIPRESENT

The infinite variety of people, things, activities, places, conditions and amounts we experience are conceptual forms or images of oneness. Each form is itself the whole of one, the infinity and omnipresence of one, of God itself. There is no other "type" of existence or form.

Oneness is always whole and complete; oneness cannot be divided and separated into parts. Each seeming "part," each form, is the whole. Each being, and each atom and cell of each being, is the whole. No part or form is what it seems to be; all is the whole. Each organ and function of each body is the whole of existence, life and vitality because God is one and omnipresent.

We can observe one object or person or one thousand, but each is the whole of God. We can have one dollar to our name or one million, but each dollar and each one million dollars are one and the same—the whole. Oneness is indivisible and inseparable, invariable, constant. How fruitful it is when we take oneness into contemplation, when we live with the truth of oneness every breath, every step, until it "takes over" and lives us. As oneness lives us, God is perfectly visible and real to us.

INDIVISIBLE AND INSEPARABLE

Oneness is indivisible and inseparable. Images or forms in and of their own selves have nothing to do with oneness. They are nothing but images or concepts within the infinite ocean of oneness, the infinite ocean of omnipresence. No one being, thing or condition *itself* is greater or lesser, more of God or less of God, more true or less true because only oneness itself is God.

Form in and of its own self is not God, but is transitory concept or belief *about* God. Each moment of our experience is transitory concept or belief—coming into experience, living for some "time," then fading into another changing or different moment.

All belief-experience consists of both good and bad—temporal, variable, good and bad form. The moment we know that God is one and invariable, indivisible, inseparable; that *oneness* is both *where* God is and *what* God is, and the moment we begin to abide in oneness, be as one, and maintain even a measure of constant conscious oneness, we are able to witness God as the forms of experience.

We witness healing and transformation of even the most dire disease or discord; we witness God as the fulfillment of all we are and have and do; we witness the image and likeness of God everywhere about. We witness the power and presence of *one* as the reality of our experience.

"I have food to eat the world knows not of." I have form unto infinity the world knows not of. I have the infinity and omnipresence of form the world knows not of because the world believes form in and of its own self to be an entity, a reality. But form of its own self is unreal.

Only God is real. Only *one is,* and one itself *is* the infinity and omnipresence of all.

Knowing this truth, abiding in conscious oneness, and letting conscious oneness *be* what I am, who I am; be the content of my mind and thought; be what I realize and recognize as my entire being and world, I *have* the infinity and omnipresent form the world knows not of.

I have the form of one, of God, the world knows nothing about.

I have the one form that is all form the world knows not of.

I have the one form that IS ITSELF *the whole of God as all.*

I have the one form that IS ITSELF *the infinity of every form in existence, freely available to me and my experience, and with which to give, serve and share, without limit,* AS LONG AS I KEEP MY MIND STAYED IN CONSCIOUS ONENESS—*in God as all, oneness as all; as long as I keep myself fueled by God itself.*

One . . . one . . . one.

APPEARANCE

Ignore the appearance of multitudinous person, place and thing. Realize that, contrary to appearance, all is one and one *only.* Never judge by form; never believe appearance in and of its own self—the seeming nature, character, quality or measure it suggests is "real." Form is never what it seems to be. All form is *the one*—the whole of one, the whole of God.

God, one, is the only being and form, indivisible and inseparable. One cannot be separated or divided, made into a variety of different and incomplete parts, categories, qualities or conditions. God, which is one, is indivisible, inseparable, invariable. There is not "more" or "less"; there is only the whole, the one, the entirety of infinity and omnipresence, omniscience and omnipotence.

God, one, is the only, and that one IS *infinity itself. Oneness* IS *infinity, and because one is all, a conscious state of oneness is a conscious experience of the infinity of all form.*

The same is true of omnipresence, omniscience and omnipotence. One *is* omnipresence, omniscience and omnipotence itself; and because one is all, a conscious state of oneness is the conscious experience of all form beheld as infinite, omnipresent, omniscient and omnipotent.

MIND-FORM

Mind is form; form is mind. Mind, being God, which is infinite, forms an infinity of oneness. Oneness is experienced as an infinity of formation, but each and every element of form is itself the whole of, the infinity and omnipresence of, one.

Form does not, nor can it, change oneness into fractions, into an actual variety, into different substance or material or character or amount or quality; mind does not change one into lesser or separate form. Form is not at all different from God. When this great truth is known and allowed to live, the infinity and freedom of form is ours in tangible and practical experience.

One is one. Nothing changes this truth. In a conscious state of oneness we have arrived at the secret place of the most high, the most one, the most God. As we abide *there* in conscious oneness and live out from it, we experience oneness as real and practical form. Our thinking is about one, not one "and," not about multiplicity.

We do not entertain the belief in difference, in more versus less, in God "and" matter. We are filled with one and oneness. We are aware of the one body and what that body is, which is one and oneness—spirit, incorporeality never anything different, never physical; not consisting of physical atoms and cells, organs and functions on which the body is dependent for its life and longevity.

Life is God, life is one, life is consciousness, and so do you see that when we are in a conscious state of oneness, we *have life.* A conscious state of oneness *is* conscious life and everything included with conscious life, which includes the conscious life of the mind, the body and all organs and functions.

The body does not have a set of different organs and functions. The body has just one, and that is God itself, oneness itself.

How do we witness that one, how do we experience the healing of a body or an organ or function which we believe to be physical and different from God or one, and on which we believe our life depends? We come to conscious oneness. In and as conscious oneness we *have* life; we *have* the healing of belief, we *have* the healing of the "physical" body—of whatever sickness or injury it may have been suffering. In the light of conscious oneness we discover that the body was not actually suffering from any sickness but the sickness of mis-identity.

MIS-IDENTITY = SUFFERING

Suffering of any category is mis-identity. Mis-identity,

once realized, leads us, sometimes by force, to God, oneness. It is our pain and our suffering, our prodigal state of being, that stirs and drives us back home to *what* God is and to *where* God is, to what and where we and all truly are—a conscious state of oneness.

In and as and through the conscious state of oneness, our conscious*ness*—our "temple"—becomes *of* God. Our reality becomes the image and likeness of God (good without opposite) instead of the image and likeness of belief.

When we realize that our consciousness, our very being or presence itself (and everything observed throughout our life) is "the temple of the living God," and that the temple is *consciousness,* it quickly clicks within us that *conscious oneness* is the secret of tangibly experiencing the oneness that God is.

In conscious oneness we let the temple of our being reveal itself to us *as* the living God. God, alive in us, alive as our conscious oneness, makes its image and likeness visible and tangible to our senses. "We" do not do it; we cannot. But God *alive in us* does; God felt happening in us does.

When we're in truthful identity, when we are in conscious oneness, we rest and let God get on with being God, let the temple of the living God *be* the vitality, visibility and tangibility of itself—just as the sun is the light and warmth of itself throughout the universe.

We let God be and see for us, and even let God heal our senses for us, heal our form, finances, conditions, places, business, relationships, neighborhood, nation and world.

The moment we realize what all is—consciousness, "the temple of the living God"—and when we then rest in that temple of conscious oneness and let God get on with being God *as* that temple, then the miracle of good is quickly evident.

Whether a single cell or an entire body of cells, a tiny

pebble or the Himalayas, a single dollar or one million dollars, a single person or 7.3 billion people, a tiny village or a bustling city, a cancer or a perfectly healthy body, *all*, despite appearance, is God—the very presence, the very living temple or consciousness of God.

All, despite appearance, despite the most persuasive belief, is God, *the* one, *the* whole, never greater or lesser, never divided or separated, never categorized, never different in nature, quality or amount, but forever *one*, God without belief, good without opposite. When we know this truth, *what* it is (oneness) and *where* it is (oneness), and then bring ourselves into a conscious state of oneness, we *have* the infinite and ever-present resources of God.

Certainly, the world knows not of these resources; the world cannot access or experience them. But even a grain of conscious oneness actually lived is greater than that which is in the world.

One with God is a majority. Even if our whole world seems to be collapsing around us, our conscious oneness with God proves that matter has no power to hinder or destroy us, and that actually our world is heaven. "As in heaven so on earth."

When we maintain ourselves in a state of conscious oneness we have the infinity and omnipresence of all form. No matter what its name or category, we have the infinity and omnipresence of all form because we know that form is not what it seems to be, but is oneness, God. Everything "connected" with each person, thing or condition is, despite appearance, oneness, spirit, God.

As long as I have that one, as long as I maintain conscious oneness, as long as I can look "out" into my world and know that I am observing just one and not many, then I have the infinity, omnipresence, power and freedom of God, good without opposite, as all form.

These infinite resources of good are at my constant and unconditional disposal because I "stay my mind on thee," because I keep myself in and being, a conscious state of oneness.

I AND EXISTENCE ARE ONE

"I and my father are one." I and my true state of being are one *because I have brought myself* to a conscious state of oneness. I have given up two-ness; I have given up multiplicity, variety, category, difference. I have given up belief, concept and false identity.

Just one; this is what I keep in mind, this is the song I keep singing within—*just one, just oneness.*

"I live and move and have my being in God." I am, my mind is, my body is, and my entire universe is (lives, moves and thinks in) oneness.

Just one, that is all. Just God. I have given up dividing and separating. I have given up believing in difference and measure, time and space, cause and effect, and now I am filled full—and I make sure that I keep filling myself full—of oneness.

I keep singing the song of oneness. I keep reminding myself of JUST ONE; not many, but ONE alone, GOD alone.

Live now, my friends, with the eternal song of oneness. *Just God . . . just spirit . . . just oneness.*

Keep your awareness filled with just one. Sing the song of oneness one thousand times a day.

One . . . one . . . one.

Then rest many times during each twenty-four hours in your attained state of conscious oneness. When you feel that conscious oneness is true; when you have for this moment attained a state of conscious oneness; when conscious oneness *feels greater* than appearance—when you feel its presence happening within—rest. This is the time, or state of being, in which to stop your effort and rest, *letting* oneness *be everything for you.*

Simply rest without thought, without concern, without effort. Rest without believing you have to "do" something, or that something material or structural has to "change" in order for harmony to prevail—in order for your health or healing to come about, for sufficient money to be available, for love to be yours, for relationship, family, home to become harmonious, for safety and security to become tangible. Forget the problem and the need. All of these are but belief and the false experience of mis-identity.

When you have attained a state of conscious oneness, rest and *let* God *be* God. *Let* God be "the temple of the living God," the temple of your living consciousness. But realize that "the temple of your living consciousness" must be God's temple, God's living consciousness which is experienced only as "you" rest and let God be for you what God-life is, what God-mind is, what God-body is, what God-thing is, what God-activity is, what God-amount is, what God-world is.

Rest and let God get on with *being God as you* and *as everything* in your experience.

Do not doubt that God *is.* Wherever you look, wherever you place your thought, wherever you go *there I am. I* am all. I am not what seems to be; I *am I alone.*

Whatever seems to be, whatever you think about, wherever you go, and whatever you do; whatever you believe has to "happen" according to appearance and human sense, is not God, is not what actually is, and is not what actually has to happen. What all actually is is God, oneness, in perfect and eternal, here-and-now order. The only thing required to tangibly experience our God-life is the filling of our senses with living God awareness.

As quickly as we have arrived at a conscious state of oneness, we can drop every belief and fear. We can rest and relax because we now know that form and condition without belief are God, the presence and formation of good. We can put down every fear and concern because we are home in the bosom of God. *There,* all we have to do is rest and freely receive.

Be still and know that I, conscious oneness, am God. And because I am all that you are—absolutely every atom, cell and fiber of you; every form and activity of your experience—you have only to let me be me.

Let me be conscious oneness throughout you. As you rest in me—in stillness, silence and receptivity—you will quickly see me as the harmony and peace of you and of your world.

You will begin to see me everywhere, as all that is. The false identities of your mind, body, and world begin to dissolve, and the boundlessness and freedom of truth emerge.

The true life, love and abundance of being and world emerge through the dissipating fog of belief the moment belief is dropped, and God, conscious oneness, is lived. The joy, fulfillment and purpose that have been clouded from experience emerge, strong and free, and often in such a rush that it seems as if the "old" you and "old" set of limiting circumstances never existed. Indeed they were never real;

they were only believed to be.

All is the whole of God—infinity and omnipresence. All that God (good) is and has is already everywhere present. God is right here where you are, the only form and condition. In the very place where a different condition seems to be, where something less than the perfection and full visibility of God seems to be, there God *actually is.*

That which has turned up as illness, disease, poverty, lack, limitation, insecurity, hate or injustice is *collective belief unwittingly accepted as real.* When we know that God is and that nothing but God is—that oneness is and nothing but oneness is—we only have to rest, and we will find that our senses become so filled with God that we cannot look anywhere into our universe and not see God.

In conscious oneness rest, and all the fruits of truth, all the awareness, life, abundance, love, and purpose of God flows forth and becomes perfectly visible and tangible. All good is evidenced already manifested and demonstrated throughout you and as everything you are and everything you do as God-form instead of belief-form.

Just one . . . just one.

This is the song I sing all day and all night.

Oneness is all; therefore oneness is who I am and what I have, my world and everything in it and of it.

Oneness is all; therefore oneness is all form and experience.

Oneness is the self I am, the mind and body I have, the world I experience.

Oneness is forever whole and complete, full of life and vi-

tality, love and joy, abundance and fulfillment.

My conscious state of oneness IS *my fulfillment of all of self, body, and world.*

My conscious state of oneness IS *my conscious experience of God being all that is.*

7

TO KNOW IS TO HAVE

TO *TRULY KNOW* IS TO *HAVE.* Knowledge is demonstration. "I and my Father are one." To claim knowledge but lack demonstration is unknowing. It is by the degree that an individual's life is fruitful, peaceful and free that you know his state of spiritual awareness. "By their fruits ye shall know them."

Truth and its fruits (demonstration) are not intellectual knowledge and understanding alone. The intellect may believe it understands an aspect of truth the first time it hears it. We may quickly "get" it. But intellectual understanding is dry and shallow ground in which the seed of truth cannot find root and soon shrivels and dies. It is only as the soil of our being is sufficiently deep and nutritious—as we begin to *feel* the truth, *feel the presence* stirring within—that we are awakening to reality and beginning to evidence God as our mind, body and world.

It is in the realization, in the *feeling* of truth that we find our freedom and fulfillment of being.

INFINITY *IS* ONENESS

God *is,* one *is.* Nothing "else" is.

God is one, and because God is all, all is one. And God, one, is spirit. Spirit is incorporeal and cannot become corporeal. Lift above corporeal awareness and begin to be aware, to think, in terms of incorporeality.

God is infinity. Hear it; emphasize the word *is.* One *is* infinity itself. No other "type" of infinity exists, nor does infinity exist anywhere else or as anything else. We cannot experience infinity unless we are experiencing oneness.

Infinity is oneness itself, God itself, spirit itself. Oneness is—itself—THE infinitude. There is no infinity outside of or other than or different from oneness itself, which is spirit or consciousness.

Spirit, consciousness, oneness, God IS ITSELF infinity.

Remember, as soon as we have one "and," as soon as we have "two," we do not have any of God, any oneness whatsoever even though we may believe we do.

Without oneness we do not have any of infinity whatsoever. We have two beliefs, neither of which is nor can be infinity. Only *one* is infinity; only God is infinity; spirit, consciousness *is itself* infinity.

Nothing but a God state of being can evidence or bring forth the infinity of form because *only God itself* is infinity, and God is *oneness.* And because God is consciousness, only a conscious state of oneness evidences the infinity of form in experience.

In the same way, God or oneness *itself is* omnipresence, omniscience and omnipotence. As soon as we have anything "additional" to one, we have no oneness, no God whatsoever, but merely two beliefs.

God is not present in experience at all as soon as we introduce an "and," a belief. Just one "and"—one belief—fills our universe with "two." It is impossible to evidence God in a state of twoness. God cannot be made into something that God is not. God cannot share itself with something "else," making a second "type" of God. It is impossible. God is the one and the only, the infinite and the omnipresent. Nothing "else" is and nothing else can be.

One *itself* is omnipresence. If we believe in the existence of something "else," that "something else" cannot possibly reveal the omnipresence of God that it truly is. The person, thing or condition believed to be something other than God cannot become evident as the wholeness and completeness—the God-form—that it actually is. Belief makes us blind to that which is, just as darkness makes us blind to the earth on which we are standing.

It is utterly impossible to see God-being and God-form when person or form is believed to be something other than God. God is infinite and omnipresent, *oneness* alone. God, oneness, cannot see two, and cannot make two into one, into God-good. No way exists to make something believed to be other than God reveal its God-quality—the health, wealth and harmony it truly is. Only one is, and only oneness sees itself.

What does oneness see itself as? *One.* As soon as we have "otherness," we do not have and cannot see God as the forms of our experience.

The same is true of omniscience. Omniscience, the all knowing, all-wise mind of God, is oneness. As soon as we have one "and," God "and," we have no oneness at all, no God at all, therefore no omniscience at all. Then it is impossible to bring forth omniscience from form or condition because omniscience is not available in an "and," in the belief in an existence other than, less than or different from God.

Equally, omnipotence *is* oneness; omnipotence *is* God. As soon as we have something "else," omnipotence is not and cannot be evident because the only omnipotence *is* oneness itself, God itself. We cannot make of God "more" than God is. If we attempt to, we just have belief, and in belief there is no omnipotence and no way of reaching omnipotence. In belief it is not possible to evidence omnipotence in or as, or governing, the forms of experience.

DETECT AND DROP SUBTLE BELIEF

We have subtle beliefs that are difficult to detect and drop, but they have to be detected and have to be dropped. They act somewhat like this: "I am spiritual being. I have heard this truth one thousand times and I intellectually understand and accept it. I am spiritual being, yes, *but at the same time I have a physical body with physical organs and functions.*" There it is, the subtle belief in twoness, in spirit "and" matter, in the incorporeal "and" the corporeal, in one "and" two or more.

The truth is, we have never had a physical body with physical organs and functions. We are spiritual being, and have only *spiritual* body, organ, function, and purpose; and that spiritual body is the body of *one.*

I am and have the one body, and that one body is spirit. As I experience my body, which until now I have believed is physical, I am experiencing nothing physical, but I am experiencing the only body that exists, which is spirit.

I am having a physical SENSE *of the spiritual body, but that sense in and of its own self is not real. It never has been real;*

it is just sense.

Sense should never have been called "physical" or "material." All is spirit; therefore all sense is spiritual. There is nothing else it can be, nothing else it is; there is no other substance or faculty from which sense is made.

We are having a corporeal sense of that which is one hundred percent incorporeal. We can call it physical or material if we insist, but that is like calling an idea a thing. An idea is not a thing; it is incorporeal.

I like to keep truth clear and distinct in my mind, and in the Miracle Self teaching. That clarity and distinction is that we are having a corporeal sense of the incorporeal, a physical or material sense of the spirit which is the all and the only. We are having a multitudinous sense of that which is one.

The corporeal sense does not *make* our experience corporeal, physical or material. Sense is nothing but sense. The totality of our experience including every form in the universe is spiritual and will forever remain so. Only spirit is; only one is. The "physical" body experience is nothing but a corporeal sense of the one spiritual body.

If we believe that we are *in truth* a spiritual being with a spiritual body, yet, *at the same time,* we have a physical body which we have to keep healthy or heal, then we cannot help but reach to God for physical help or healing. We believe that if only we can reach high enough or effectively enough in spirit, we will receive a physical healing. "Ye ask, and receive not, because ye are ask amiss."

As soon as we have spiritual discernment, we realize that we cannot have a "physical" healing. We cannot expect the healing of a physical body, organ or function because physicality does not exist. Physicality is just a *sense* of that which is one hundred percent spirit. The secret then, is to heal *sense.*

A continued expectation that God can provide us with physical healing is what blocks the healing. Our true body experience, that of spiritual form and faculty, cannot "get through" as long as we continue to believe that the physical is real in and of its own self. Nothing physical exists; therefore there is nothing physical to heal. The only body is the spiritual body.

When we realize this great truth, when we come to oneness and realize that oneness *is,* and then rest impersonally and receptively in that *is,* letting it reveal the truthful, spiritual body, we quickly experience the transformation (healing) of the bodily experience.

Can you hear it clearly? Oneness *is.* Oneness *itself is.* Oneness *itself is life.* Oneness itself *is the body.* It does not matter that we have a corporeal or physical sense. It does not matter that corporeal or physical sense makes it *appear* as if our body is made up of many vital organs and functions as long as we can *ignore what appears to be.* Ignore the complexity of appearance and realize that the body is spirit itself, oneness itself, forever whole, healthy and vital.

Oneness *is* the body. To have a conscious experience of our true body we have to have a conscious experience of oneness. Oneness is the one form of the body. There are not different body forms or functions; oneness is the only, the one form and function. No "part" is more or less vital. Oneness is the entirety of the body, all "parts" being equal and full of God—the one organ, the one function, the one vitality, the one purpose, the omnipresent body.

Realize that oneness is spirit, God, and is eternal, invariable, inseparable—unchanging and indivisible oneness. Oneness does not and cannot divide itself into many. Oneness *is,* and is the only *is.* The body is that.

FREELY RECEIVE YOUR HEALTH

If you can hear this, then no matter what state of health your body seems to be in at this moment, you can rest in oneness and discover its health.

Do not fall foul of the pairs of opposites and believe that poor physical health "needs God" but good health does not. This pairs-of-opposites belief about the state of the body is a dream state of existence. Whether the body is physically healthy or unhealthy, the realization of its being spiritual lifts it from belief (the pairs of opposites) into truth (health *without* opposite).

If we can ignore its apparent healthy or unhealthy physical state and realize that the *true* body is a conscious state of oneness, then we will go to oneness, abide and rest in oneness, and let oneness reveal to us, fill our senses with, fill our experience full of itself—the living God, the living truth; the living life, the living body. Very quickly then we discover that our body is not only healed but is stronger, more youthful, vital, beautiful, and eternal.

But we must stop seeking and expecting or even hoping for a physical transformation. Stop it—the physical does not exist in God. The physical is merely sense. If we carry on believing the physical, we fall right into that statement that tells us, Ye ask [seek], and receive not, because ye ask amiss. Why or how do we seek amiss? Because we are seeking *physical* healing or transformation.

In the same way, the spiritual mind is not buried deep within our "mental" mind, unobtainable except to the spiritual few, leaving the rest of us struggling for spiritual awareness—struggling to see and think about God, to be aware of God. There is no truth to such a belief, and if we carry on believing it, we will carry on struggling. It is as simple is that. Whatever we carry on believing, we carry on struggling with. There is no way out of belief except to drop it and start living in truth. Drop belief now and forever, lift up into truth (into oneness) and there begin to live the freedoms of the limitless life.

GOD DOES NOT FAVOR THE PERSONAL SELF

God is God alone and cannot be used to benefit a belief in a personal self. The personal self will forever fail in its attempt to use God because there is not a personal you, me or anyone *in* God. Because God is all, only God can be.

The personal self and its entire universe exists as *belief* alone. The mind of God is full of just one thing and that is God itself, and God itself does not have humanity, mentality, physicality, materiality or personal selves in it whatsoever.

The mind of God is full of God awareness, full of God being and form which is oneness, equally and fully present everywhere at the same time—never personal, never local, never finite, never selfish.

All is God and of God. The spiritual mind (our true mind) is aware of God alone, spirit alone, oneness alone. The spiritual mind is aware of infinity, omnipresence, omniscience, omnipotence, eternity alone—the formless form, the one universal form, oneness without otherness; spirit alone. This is the mind of God.

We cannot "use" the mind of God to gain personal good. There isn't any personal good in God because there is no personal self in God. The only good is God-good; the only truth is God-truth; the only presence is God-presence, the only form is God-form. And the only God there is is infinite, omnipresent; omni-being, omni-form, omni-good.

"God saw everything that he had made and, behold, it was very good." Note the words carefully: "he *had* made" and "*it* was very good." Why past tense and singular? God is the *eternal one* unchanging existence. Everything of God, therefore of all, is that one, eternal, unchanging existence; the one infinity, omnipresence, omniscience, omnipotence, eternity.

Experience is the ceaseless unfolding awareness of God as one, as all formation, of good omnipresent and never-ending, of good without opposite unfolding moment by moment, of "earth as it is in heaven."

When we drop personal sense (belief) and lift into and live in oneness, never hoping for anything physical or material "from" oneness, never hoping for a physical or material "result" from God, but are *satisfied with God itself,* then our whole being is empty of self and free in spirit, and quickly fills with the light of spirit. In such a spiritualized state of being we gaze into and "out" at our bodies and worlds and discover the image and likeness of oneness, God. All is as it is and eternally has been; as God "has made" it—"very good."

None is personal, physical, material or corporeal. All is spirit and spiritual, and when we know this, we never again seek any "thing" or "condition." We seek God, find God, and abide in God (oneness). Once we are there, we are doing the single greatest thing in the kingdom of heaven, and that is resting in and as impersonal receptivity, *letting* the temple of the living God reveal its universe to us. We are letting God reveal its image and likeness—its activity, form, amount, body, business, family, home, neighborhood, nation and earth—*as it is,* which is God, oneness, spirit.

As we lift into and abide in oneness, as we rest and relax and let oneness live our life, live our awareness, live our mind, body and world *for us,* then we discover that "the earth is the Lord's and the fullness thereof"; then we discover that "the earth is full of the goodness of God"; then we discover that there never was a personal I, me or mine. All this time there has been only God, and now we are witnessing it.

We never again seek anything material when we have discovered the truth of oneness, abide in it and let it live us. Why would we seek a little portion of good matter when our whole self-body-universe is full of infinity; and we know it, we see it, we witness it, we rejoice in it and with it, we get busy giving and sharing the infinity and the omnipresence of it to all who come to partake?

In the same way, oneness *is* wealth. Oneness itself is abundance, prosperity, limitlessness of all form because all form is the one form. Oneness itself is wealth infinite, abundance infinite; prosperity, success, achievement infinite, without condition.

The only requirement is to stop believing that there is spiritual wealth within us, *and* a material form of money "out there."

There is no spirit "and," one "and." I have not met more than two or three students who, when belief presses hard enough, are able to rest secure in the realization that God itself is the infinity and omnipresence of wealth, and is ever-present, real and practical. Most are stuck believing that there is spirit, the one true form of wealth, "and" material money. Most believe that sufficient spiritual realization will "cause" material money to become "manifested" or "demonstrated" for them. If we still expect our spiritual awareness to produce a material result, we will continue to fail. Why? We are believing in twoness instead of oneness. We have a divided consciousness, and a divided consciousness cannot witness oneness. "Every kingdom divided against itself is brought to desolation; and every city or house divided against itself shall not stand."

In a divided consciousness our seeking is two-minded,

dual. We seek God and expect matter. We seek spirit and expect it to appear physically; we seek oneness and expect it to appear in forms that oneness is not. This is impossible. There *is no* human being with physical and material needs. There is no physical, material, corporeal being or thing. There is only one, and that one is spirit which is forever whole and complete; and *is itself the infinity of its form.*

We witness the one form as the infinity of all experienced form as soon as we know the truth of oneness, stay in conscious oneness, and (most importantly) once we are there, rest, and experience *spiritual* satisfaction, *spiritual* formation—spiritual life, spiritual wealth and prosperity.

This is how spiritual fulfillment is lived. Once we live as and in and by spirit, and as we expect nothing but spiritual good, realizing that there simply isn't any matter, humanity or physicality, but that all forms of corporeal experience, despite the way they appear to be, are the *one form* which is spirit itself, then we experience the fullness of spiritual form as the multiple variety of experienced form.

To the outsider these look as if they are different and separate, greater and lesser, here-and-there forms of good, but we know they are not. They are *the one* witnessed *as one* in a boundless variety of formation.

All the supposed different formations are not different at all. They are the *one formation* simply appearing to be a universe of variety. Realize that your wealth, your infinite and omnipresent abundance of good form, including dollars, *is oneness.* When you reach the place (state) of conscious oneness and are letting it live you, you *have* and *own* the conscious experience of oneness being the omnipresence of all the wealth in existence.

You are not separate from wealth. Wealth is not out there somewhere, different, separate and apart from you.

Wealth is not, and cannot be, separate and apart from you, hard to make or earn or win, leaving you in want and need. You have never been required to work for wealth. Wealth—boundless and unconditional in all its form, including the form of money—is oneness itself.

Go to oneness. Become conscious of one and realize that *one* is *all.* Nothing exists but one, God. Realize this truth and then rest in oneness and let your temple—your consciousness—be filled with the living God, the living awareness, the living visibility, the living tangibility; the fully manifested and demonstrated wealth unto infinity. Limitless wealth is one with you, one *as* you. *Oneness itself*—not oneness changing itself into material wealth, but oneness itself.

Realize it forevermore. There is no material wealth (nor is there material anything). Only one is, only oneness is, only God is, only spirit is.

Oneness *is itself* your abundance and immediacy of wealth. Can you hear that? If you can, or when you can, you will never again feel poor or in lack. You will never again seek a dollar. You will never again seek a human client, customer, patient or student. You will never again seek a loan, and you will never need to. Oneness is wealth in all its ways—oneness itself.

Also, when you know this great truth, you will discover many ways and forms and activities of wealth that you didn't know existed. God is infinite and because God is wealth, wealth is infinite. Wealth is not just a dollar. Wealth includes dollars but also includes an infinite number of other ways and forms of opportunity, success and prosperity. You start noticing them opening up and presenting themselves to you when you realize that wealth—tangible, practical, visible wealth—is oneness itself. You quickly discover the infinite ways and forms of wealth, and the omnipresence of wealth including dollars, when know and abide in and let oneness itself, be your wealth.

Oneness itself is home. There is no other type of home. There is not a spiritual home existing within us somewhere, ethereal and impractical "and" a material, structural home. Until we know this we cannot help the subtle expectation of spirit producing a material home for us. There isn't a material home; there isn't a material anything. Only spirit is.

When you realize that oneness *itself* is home, that consciously experienced oneness is consciously experienced home (the practical formation of home), you simply rest in and experience the form of oneness presenting itself to you as a fulfilling home. Oneness is whole and complete home—even the very name or number on the front door.

When we realize that conscious oneness is home, and that conscious oneness does not contain physicality, locality, neighborhood, size, number or name in it, but is the infinity and omnipresence of oneness, we equally realize the reality and practicality of oneness being the tangible form of home.

If you will just know this, lift up into oneness and stop your effort in the physical, stop your effort for certain locality, certain position, certain size, all to be achieved by a certain time, and realize that (literally) oneness itself *is* home; and if you will restfully abide in the home of oneness, letting oneness *itself* live and breathe as your home, then, if you need a new experience of home, its palpable form will quickly present itself.

It is present already. You have the keys and you have the directions. All is *I,* conscious oneness. Go to *it,* abide in *it,* and *let it show itself* as your corporeal sense, a "wonder to behold." Then, before you know it, you have your corporeally-sensed, new and fulfilling home.

LOVE AND RELATIONSHIP

"God is love." How many of the world's spiritual devotees know this truth and repeatedly affirm it, yet are still searching for love?

God is love; there is not a higher truth. And because God is all, love is all. Love is every being and every breath and cell of every being; love is in the earth and in the air. Love is omnipresent because God is omnipresent and God is love. However, until it is realized that God is consciousness and God is one, all the knowledge and affirmation about God being love does not *evidence* love.

Love is conscious oneness itself; relationship is conscious oneness itself. If we have fallen into the subtle trap of believing that the love that God is is buried deep within somewhere and that—if it can be tapped into by sufficiently realizing God as love, meditating on love and sitting in the silence of love—love will produce loving *human* relationships, we will continue to lack love. We "seek amiss," and if we seek amiss we do not *have,* we do not *evidence,* we do not *experience.*

We have to awaken to the truth that God is love, and that because God is *consciousness* and *one,* love is the experience and form of conscious oneness itself.

Oneness *itself* is love and loving relationship—the relationship of and with oneness. When we have lifted into a conscious state of oneness and abide there, letting oneness live us, we *have love* in all its being and form, and *are having* the one true relationship. We *are in* the relationship, the one and only relationship. We do not need any other category of relationship—a "human" category of relationship—because there is none. God is the one and the only, because God is all. If we still believe there is an additional type of relationship to be had, or that love, once experienced spiritually, must be fulfilled humanly, we have still not understood God, consciousness, oneness. We are still mis-identifying what God is, therefore all that we, love and relationship are.

All is God; therefore all is love. To experience love and to have loving relationship, which is to have true relationship, we have to be love, which is to be the conscious oneness that God (love) is. Then the love that God is becomes the love that we are. The love that God is, everywhere present, becomes our ever-present and giving nature. When we are in a state of conscious oneness, the love that God is fills our senses, becomes our nature, and animates our expression. All in our body and world is then "in love with us," and we with it. Love abounds because we are *being love,* within and without, as we live and move and have our being in a state of conscious oneness.

Oneness itself *is* love; oneness itself *is* relationship; and because oneness is God, the relationship of oneness is infallibly lov*ing.*

When we have the relationship of oneness we *have* love throughout our universe. As we let love live itself as us, we quickly find ourselves with a corporeal sense of the one loving relationship as that which, to material sense, looks like a deeply loving human relationship. But the "human" relationship is only the form made evident as love itself. When we are in our conscious state of oneness, love itself has the space and freedom within us to live, to *be,* to be evident, vital. The form is not "human" although it appears to be. In reality it is the relationship of oneness, the relationship of God evident "in the world."

Oneness itself is love. There is no other experience of true love. The only "other" experience of love is believed love. Believed love is never God love because God love is one love, the *oneness* of being which is the one love itself.

If we believe true love exists in our *human* relationships we are mistaken. God has no humanity in it; therefore true love cannot exist among humans. Humanity believes relationship is the bond between two or more people, but *God* is the only being; therefore the only true love, the only true relationship, is the love and relationship of oneness. God-love *appears* as and between two or more. But the way true love appears is as and "through" the relationship of oneness.

Any appearance, if believed to be a person, a relationship, an entity or a condition in and of its own self, is not God. Only *God* exists, and God is one; therefore only in conscious oneness, and in the experience of oneness living us, do we have love and loving relationship appearing as the love "between" two or more people. The image and likeness of the relationship of oneness appears to be loving human relationship.

In the same way, peace is oneness itself, harmony is oneness itself; justice and union between people and nations is oneness itself. If we attempt to use God to bring forth harmony, peace, morality, justice and union between people and nations we will forever fail. It cannot be done. History has proven it. Only *oneness itself is* harmony, peace, morality, justice and union. Oneness itself cannot "produce" these among humans. Oneness itself *is* these.

Can you hear it? Oneness itself *is* these. Only when we have the experience of conscious oneness itself do we *have* the experience of good itself. We *have* the tangible experience of peace, harmony, love, union, justice, morality and fulfillment *when we are having* the experience of conscious oneness.

EXPERIENCE THE LIFE OF GOD

Oneness itself is the one real, one practical, one palpably experienced life of God on earth. Oneness itself is "earth as it is in heaven." There is no other true experience, true life, true body or true world.

God is omnipresence and is already where I am; and because God is all, all that I experience must be realized as omnipresence and already existent where I am.

Life is omnipresence and is already where I am. Infinite wealth and fulfillment are omnipresence and are already where I am.

Life is omnipresence and is already where I am, what I am and what I have. I do not need to seek God, to seek health, to seek love, to seek peace, to seek prosperity. If I seek these, I believe they are not already present, not where I am, not what I am, not what I have. But God and all that God is is omnipresent and is forever where I am.

I do not have to seek any good thing or condition; I simply have to be conscious of them, which means conscious of what they are, which is CONSCIOUS ONENESS, *and then abide in that conscious oneness to* HAVE *all the life, all the wealth and all the harmony I could ever wish for or need, with twelve baskets full left over.*

Abiding in conscious oneness, I need only rest and *let* the omnipresent life which is already where I am, let the omnipresent wealth which is already where I am, let the omnipresence of love, peace, harmony, business, family and neighborhood which is already where I am live itself "for me."

I need only let the living oneness be itself as me, fill my consciousness; fill my senses full of itself, fill my whole universe full of itself, its oneness. Then I *have* the image and likeness of all the life, love, peace and harmony that God is. All that God is and has is now real and practical, visible and tangible in experience. "All things are yours."

All that God is and has—all that oneness, infinity, omnipresence, omniscience and omnipotence is and has—is ours *as* worldly form. We *have* the image and likeness of God throughout experience because we are living oneness happening.

THE GREAT SECRET

One is—just one. This is the great secret. Conscious oneness is our true state of being, our infinity of being, our God state; the state of being that provides our experience with the freedom of the world's true good.

Conscious oneness is what we abide in, where we abide, and what *lives us* as we rest in oneness simply beholding God in action throughout our experience.

In our rested and receptive state of conscious oneness, we behold God filling, transforming, healing, saving all in our world, and even raising from the dead that which to belief seems to have lost life.

If we quickly lift into and maintain even the least degree of true conscious oneness—"the least in the kingdom of heaven"—and abide in that "least" of oneness, letting *it* fill our being, *be* our being, *live* our mind, body and world *for us,* all we need do is *behold* the miracle of God as our fulfilled corporeal sense, and then freely and joyously serve our world with the abundant good with which we are blessed.

Let God *be God as itself* as us. Let one *be one* as us, so that we never again misidentify ourselves, others or anything of our world; so that we expect the fulfillment of God or one and nothing other, nothing different, nothing less. Then we are free, we are truthful being, and we are able to say (even by a small degree) with Saint Paul, "I live, yet not I, Christ [spirit, oneness] lives my life."

I do not have any life but God, one, Christ, Buddha, spirit. What I am and have is oneness, nothing else. And I know that *oneness* is the finished kingdom, the whole, perfect and purposeful life I am, the mind I have, the body I have, and the universe I experience, including every being and form in it.

In a conscious state of oneness, all we have to do to tangibly experience the true purpose and fulfillment of being is to stay in oneness, abide morning, noon and night in oneness, and most importantly, to *let* oneness live *itself* as and through us. Then we discover that we have the image and likeness of oneness populating our world; we have the image and likeness of God populating our mind as the one mind, our thought as the one thought, and our body as the one body (including the one organ, function and purpose). Only then can we stand strong in our freedom and purpose of being, and, in that strength, be the god of our universe.

We are fulfilling the reason we are alive on earth. We are the light of spirit, the "children" of God right here on earth. We are that presence that enables truth to be revealed.

Wherever we are, in a God-state of being, there God is evident. We are the spiritual substance that feeds the multitudes, that saves and comforts those who are unsafe or fearful, that heals the sick and the dying. We are the flame of truth that sparks spiritual awakening in individuals who are ready and willing to leave the dream state and discover their truth. We are the love and protection that allow "human" beings to release what they are holding onto, and discover that their existence is infinitely greater, more extraordinary and more purposeful than it has been believed to be.

One is; one itself is. Never again accept any person, thing or circumstance to be a reality, an entity, in and of its own self. Realize and acknowledge all as *the one* that is God, "within" and "without." Once you have one as all, you have the freedom and power of one as all; you have the infinity and omnipresence of God, of the kingdom of heaven right here as earth.

"In earth as it is in heaven"—you, me and all as we are in heaven, in oneness, in truth.

8

GOOD IS WHERE I AM

God is omnipresence and is already where I am; and because God is all, all good is omnipresence and is already where I am.

YOUR GOOD AND PERFECT FULFILLMENT, in all categories of experience, is omnipresence and is already where you are.

That good and perfect fulfillment is spirit, oneness. Spirit and spiritual being are what you are, what your body is; what money is, what love and relationship are, what family and home are, what your universe of form is no matter what the name, shape, size, location or activity of it is.

All is spirit, one; all form is spirit, one. There is none else. We simply have a corporeal (material, physical, objective) *sense* of that which is one hundred percent spirit and oneness.

Even that which is sensed as disease, lack, limit, disharmony or dissatisfaction is *spirit and spiritual* because only spirit is. These are just as spiritual as their opposites: health, wealth, freedom, harmony and fulfillment. Nothing either good or bad is material or physical as it seems to be, but is spirit and spiritual because spirit is the only existence, the only being, presence and form, the only activity.

If God is all, and God is good without opposite, what is our experience of good versus bad? *Our mis-identified state of being, or awareness.*

The only sickness, poverty, starvation, disharmony, injustice, immorality, war or dissatisfaction is *a lack of God awareness.* "If you do not know yourselves, then you dwell in poverty, and you are poverty." With even a grain of true spiritual awareness—the "least in the kingdom of heaven"—belief dissolves, and God, true good, is revealed.

Belief is experience. As lifted spiritual awareness dissolves belief, disease, lack, limitation and discord dissolve to reveal health, prosperity, and harmony. With a grain of true spiritual awareness, false experience is dissolved because false experience is simply false sense—a lack of spiritual sense.

There is no *actual* lack, division, separation or isolation from God, good. There is only God, and God is forever omnipresent, already where you are. *All God formation is already where you are and is the only you and the only formation.*

Right where you are this minute, this *now,* stands your perfect and eternal spiritual body. Nothing is wrong with the spiritual body. The body cannot be (and is not now) in any way ill, diseased, injured or dysfunctional. Nothing can touch or affect the body in the slightest because it is spirit not matter, not physicality. But a lack, or "poverty," of spiritual awareness leaves us and our experience of the body in the dark. That dark *is* the experience of illness, disease, injury, old age and death.

You are experiencing your spiritual body this minute. You always have. *But* you have believed the body to be physical.

From the moment of conception we have been swamped by collective belief in the physical and we have unwittingly accepted it. But belief in the physical, structural body never has been truth. Belief is never truth. Belief is belief alone.

The body is spirit and spiritual—this very body we experience. All form is spirit and spiritual. There is not a single physical body walking the earth; there is not a single material formation on earth. All being, body, object and condition are spirit and spiritual, not the believed physical or material formation they seem to be.

It is only as we believe the body to be physical that we suffer. It is only belief in the physical that leaves the body exposed and receptive to everything belief contains—the whole gamut of both good and bad.

We have all experienced it. Our body can be healthy and youthful, strong and energetic throughout our teens, twenties, thirties and forties, but then, for most, it starts to become "old." Its joints become stiff and painful, its hair turns grey, its skin begins to dry and wrinkle. The aging process sets in and continues until the body eventually becomes decrepit and dies.

We also know and may have experienced the body being healthy and vital one day and sick, diseased or injured the next. Out of "nowhere" come these experiences. The gamut of belief is the seemingly endless range of good and bad the human race experiences. It is the belief in God "and"—God *and* humanity, spirit *and* matter, the incorporeal *and* the corporeal, truth *and* untruth.

As soon as we discover that only God is, that only spirit and truth are; that we and our body are one hundred percent spirit, we begin to experience our true body, and if needed, its healing. The body fills with new life and vitality, lifts out of its false state of sickness or disease, and stands upright and healthy—just as a flower once deprived of water and nutrition and now provided with them, quickly recovers, stands up, and once again gives of its beauty and fragrance.

Every day people reach out for healing. If they are receptive and are sufficiently able to let go of belief, they have their healing in minutes or within a few hours. For some it takes a few days or weeks. Those who are not as spiritually receptive and cannot yet let go take longer, sometimes many weeks or even months. Those who are not spiritually receptive, who are unwittingly (or stubbornly) convinced of their personal selves and personal problem may not heal at all. These dear people return for healing again and again, but they cannot accept it. The light of truth cannot find entry into the stubborn personal belief any more than sunlight can find entry into tightly shuttered windows.

Nothing blocks our full and natural healing *except* our own stubborn belief that the body is physical and is in need of physical healing, *and* the belief that God or spirit will heal the physical.

This minute your whole and perfect spiritual body exists right where the physical seems to be. God is omnipresence and is already and forever in perfect order and formation as you, me and all. God and form are *one,* and because God is the only, all form is God. The "physical, material" form we sense is actually God form, spiritual form, because only God or spirit is.

Experiencing God form is all a matter of truthful identity; our suffering is a matter of mis-identity.

As soon as we mis-identify by believing in an existence which is less than or different from God or oneness, we suffer it. We are the prodigal, wandering away from the Father's house, away from the consciousness of oneness into the belief of multiplicity—God "and."

Life is omnipresence and is already where you are; and besides that one life there is none else. The body is the body of life itself—the temple of the living God. It is never ill, diseased or injured. But in order to experience that truthful body, we must know what it is, which is spirit, and what its functionality is, which is spiritual, and then *let spirit live as our body.* If you can hear this you are fast becoming free. Freedom does not take long because if you can hear that the body is spirit; that spirit is the only power, presence, function and form; and that spirit maintains *itself,* you rest and relax and let spirit do all the "work" of healing and revealing the whole and healthy body it is.

SELF-MAINTAINED SPIRITUAL BODY

We cannot maintain spirit and the spiritual body. Spirit maintains itself. Spirit *is,* and is the only *is,* and is in a constant state of *is,* never defaulting.

Spirit IS and is self-complete, self-contained and self-maintained.

Belief, personal sense, cannot be spiritual. Belief contains no access to spiritual power or experience. *Only spirit is.* When "we" give up the attempt to maintain our body's health or to "use" spiritual power to bring forth its healing and, instead, let spirit live and maintain its own body, our sense quickly picks up its true health and vitality. Sense is healed of the belief that binds it, and becomes free to evidence the spiritual body as it is.

Certainly, the body continues to *seem* to have corporeal

form and function, but we know that corporeal sense is sense alone, and that reality, the incorporeal, is the body being experienced.

Physicality is never again, to us, believed to be real of itself. We know belief in the physical to be a lie—in fact both the liar and the lie. As we maintain this realization, drop the lie, remain in a conscious state of oneness—a conscious state of *spiritual* self, *spiritual* body—letting spirit live as self, as body, we quickly discover that we have no illness, disease or decrepitude, and are strong and vital, whole and healthy. Our healing is complete, and our true, healthy state sustains itself.

Others may call it a miracle, but we understand that the body is spiritual. As we let spirit shine "through" our stillness and receptivity, it is not surprising that health, vitality and youthfulness become our bodily experience because these are the body's only truth.

Just as the sunbeam must know that the sun itself is its life and body and let the sun live it, so we must know that our body is not what it seems to be—not physical, but spiritual—and then let spirit *be* our life and body. If the sunbeam fell foul of the belief that it had a personal, separate, life, and then attempted to maintain it, how quickly it would become cold and dark; how quickly it would begin suffering a thousand ills. And because it believed itself to be a personal identity in a universe of other entities, it would quickly give names to its different categories of suffering. *Cold* would be one, but there are a thousand degrees of cold so a thousand different names would evolve for the ailment *cold. Dark* would be another, so a thousand different names would be born for the thousand degrees of darkness.

Sound familiar? The human race suffers from thousands of different ailments, each with a different or derivative name—illness, disease, lack, limitation, poverty, immorality, injustice, greed, racism, insecurity, fear, depression, unworthiness. Every human good has an opposite, the last and most severe of which is death. But not one human ailment is accurately identified or understood until it is discovered to be *belief.*

Belief is the "root of all evil," the belief that existence contains God "and"—God "and" humanity, God "and" the universe including everything in and of it (self, mind, body, thing, place, amount, activity, cause, effect, time, space). The moment we realize that God is all and stop mis-identifying, not only ourselves and our bodies, but our universe and everything it contains, and live as and by God alone, all human disease dissolves as naturally as ice cubes in the sun. Why? They never were real, never were actual entities. They were just belief, and because belief is nothing *but belief,* as soon as the presence of truth arrives on the scene belief and its form dissolve.

The question is, how much do you still believe in the personal self, in the physical and material, in the problem that bothers you, and a solution that will free you? By what degree do you still believe that that which *appears to be* is real in itself? How much do you still want to replace bad with good, one condition with its opposite?

The degree of belief we hold onto will at best slow down our experience of wholeness, harmony and freedom, at worst block it. Belief is the root of all problems, even the problem of "good" humanity (every human good having an opposite), and that belief is that we and our world are different and separate from God.

FEEL THE PRESENCE

Right where you are (despite what seems to be) the wholeness, harmony, abundance, peace and freedom of

God exist in tangible earth (objective) form.

Feel the presence of the spiritual self, body and earth "happening," welling up within and flooding your senses, as you contemplate the wondrous truth of God being all.

Gently realize that your spiritual body exists in the most real and practical form and function. You sense that reality as being "physical," but now, knowing its truth, rest and relax from the physical sense and turn your attention within, to one, to spirit. *There* discover your real body in all its strength and perfection. It will speak to you; it will reveal its truth. Nothing can stop it from doing so once you know its truth and open your senses to it. Just be still, silent and receptive to its spiritual presence.

In your rest and relaxation, and your turning to spirit, you begin to *feel* the spiritual body becoming tangible. Its reality floods your awareness, sometimes very gently and subtly, sometimes as a rush. You begin to feel that "something" happening within, something very beautiful, releasing, comforting, peaceful, warm. You feel relieved and saved from the physical, and free (healed) in spirit—and you *are.* This is your spiritual body being tangibly experienced.

Slowly, deliberately, spaciously contemplate—

Rest . . . relax . . . and gently bring your awareness to one, just one; to God alone, spirit alone, one alone.

"Be still, and know that I am God." Be still, and know that I, consciousness itself, am the spiritual body, the only body you have, the one body.

In your rested and relaxed state, begin to feel your spiritual self and spiritual body—your one true self and body.

It is not a physical feeling. Belief may call the feeling of spirit intangible. It is a feeling of peace or warmth or release and relief stirring within, "happening" within, flooding your senses, first in what seems to be deep within, then flowing throughout and "beyond" you.

You may feel it as light, or a sense of release, or heat, or bliss, relief and freedom from the physical, worldly sense; from the burdens of "human" mind, body and world—even from its "good." You begin to experience a good far greater and more permanent than any previously known.

Your spiritual self, body and world are greater than any physical sense can be. "He that is least in the kingdom of heaven is greater than he [that is most in the world]."

Rest, relax; begin to experience yourself by FEELING *instead of by thinking or by physical testimony.*

Relax and release your entire mental and physical sense. In your relaxed and rested state you "open out a way for the imprisoned splendor to escape"; you open out a way for the spiritual self, body and world to become real, tangible and visible in your experience. It has always been present, but now you are opening your senses to it, and are beginning to experience its reality.

Feel the peace, feel the sense of release or relief, feel that "something" peaceful or releasing or relieving happening within which has nothing to do with "your" making it happen, but which is happening despite you. It happens as you simply rest and relax the mental and physical sense, as you let go of everything of "you" and give the entirety of yourself to spirit.

Rest . . . relax . . . let go . . . be open and receptive; that is all.

You may feel the presence in a certain area of your physical sense of the body—in your chest area, your stomach, your shoulders, your forehead or around your whole head. You may feel a spaciousness in and around you; you may feel a gentle tingling sensation or a sense of "presence" in your arms or hands, chest or tummy, your legs.

However it feels, it is the spiritual self, body and world being tangibly felt. It is God itself being felt and palpably experienced.

But remember, it is not an inner, separate, different or ethereal God—there is no such God. It is the very "I" of you, the very god-being that you are. "Is it not written in your law [that] ye are gods?" Yes, the very god that you are, the very truth that you are—the spiritual self, spiritual body; the spiritual world and universe and all in it; this is what you are feeling.

You are feeling the infinity, omnipresence and eternity of the God-body. As you feel it happening, know that you are safe and secure from the world's beliefs, ills, limitations and threats. You are in the arms of the divine. You, your body and world are filled with, and being, the omnipresent form of God. You are divinely protected and free "in earth [tangible experience] as it is in heaven."

As you meditate in this way, *feeling* the presence of God throughout you, you *have* your truth; you *have* your healing and wholeness. "Have" versus "have not" has no existence in God. In God only the *oneness* of God exists.

But remember, without the *conscious awareness* and *feeling* of God happening within, you do not experience the God-health and -harmony which you are and have in truth. You are and have it, but you are unaware of it, and because awareness and experience are one, if you do not live with the awareness, the feeling of God taking place within, it seems, to objective sense testimony, as if you do not have God. Lacking the sense testimony of God, you get busy seeking that which you already are and have, which, of course, leads to failure.

The moment you awaken to the truth of oneness (the truth that there is but one life, one being, one presence, one body—that being God) and the moment you maintain your awareness of this truth and devote more daily periods of time to sitting in a quiet place, silently and receptively, letting God be God as God for God, you discover your senses more palpably filled with God. The senses filled with God are clarity of being, clarity of seeing, clarity of body, organ and function, clarity of world and everything of the world.

This clarity *is* the healing and the health, the vitality and youthfulness, the love, wealth, and harmony of experience. Filled with God awareness and feeling the presence, you *have* life in all its glorious, truthful form.

FROM STRUCTURAL TO SPIRITUAL

You are lifting and transforming your awareness of reality from physical-material-structural, to spiritual. You are awakening to the truth and logic that if spirit is the only existence, then spirit must be, and *is,* the one reality. You are adjusting your senses to perceive spirit, not matter, as reality and to live by the feeling of spirit "happening"—actually experienced—as your self, your mind, your body, and your entire world and universe.

You know that *oneness is that,* that oneness *is* God, *is* spirit. You know that oneness is where and what your entire harmonious life is, your entire healthy body is, and your entire fulfilled world is. There is no "more" or "better" to gain, to become aware of, or to demonstrate. Oneness is *where* and *what* your entire here-and-now truth is—the tangibility and reality of it, the visibility of it, the fully manifested and demonstrated, palpable experience of it.

Oneness is.

Oneness is itself my god-self.

Oneness is itself my spiritual body.

Oneness is itself my spiritual universe and every form of it, with all the beauty, bounty, purpose, pleasure and freedom of God showing forth as my every step, filling my every thought, being my every experience.

Oneness is that. Oneness *itself* is that, and as we bring ourselves to and maintain ourselves in a conscious state of oneness we *have* the treasures of God in earthly reality. They are abundant at every step and fill every thought and experience because we now know that oneness *is* infinity, omnipresence, eternity—all that God is and has. Oneness *is* our infinite, omnipresent and eternal all-of-all.

Rest . . . relax . . . bathe in the experience of God happening as all that you are, all that your mind is, all that your body is, all that your world is—every form, activity, amount, place and condition of it.

Rest . . . relax . . . and bathe in its "happening."

Rest, relax, and feel *your temple—your whole self and all that self includes—filled with God.*

Feel God dwelling throughout your consciousness,

throughout your temple, throughout the entirety of your tangible experience.

Feel God dwelling in and throughout your being and your world. Feel God being all. Let go of all belief in an inner versus and outer, an ethereal versus a structural, an incorporeal versus a corporeal. Feel the oneness of truth.

Feel God dwelling in you, animating you. Feel God being your God, your truth, your savior, your healer, your safety and protection. Feel God being the light of truth, the infinity, omniscience and omnipotence of your mind, body and of every worldly form.

Feel God being you, filling you, being all things, activity and function of your existence; BEING ITS *image and likeness as all form, all being, all amount, all circumstance, all place and condition* FOR YOU *as you simply rest and relax in a conscious state of oneness,* BEHOLDING *all that God is and has happening throughout your universe.*

You do not expect spiritual experience to transform or heal "physical" discord. You do not expect the experience of the spiritual body to heal a "physical body" or "physical illness or disease." You do not expect to heal a sick or broken "physical" body, an aged or decrepit "physical" body. You have awakened sufficiently and expect the experience of the spiritual body to dissipate the physical *sense* (belief) of reality, to reveal the spiritual as the one reality.

As light dissipates dark, spiritual illumination dissipates belief. As dark is not a reality, not an entity in and of its own self, but is simply a lack of light, so belief and belief-forms are unreal, not actual entities, but merely a lack of spiritual sense.

LIGHT DOES NOT HEAL DARK

Light does not heal dark. That which is unreal does not require healing. Light *dissipates dark* to reveal the presence of itself.

In this way, as we bathe in the experience of the spiritual self, the spiritual body, the spiritual world and expect *spiritual* transformation and fulfillment, *spiritual* tangibility and reality (never physical) we very soon discover—as long as we maintain a conscious state of oneness and regularly devote ourselves to the actual experience of oneness happening in and throughout us—that the spiritual mind, body and world have become our new reality.

It is not new in actuality, but new to our awareness. Our new awareness becomes evident and real as that which, previously, we described as the physical.

THE DEMONSTRATION OF GOD

The feeling, the experience of oneness happening, of God happening within us and throughout us is the "realization of God" or the "demonstration of God."

As soon as we have the demonstration of God our healing is complete. As we know this, therefore stop looking and waiting for something "else" to happen in the "outer"—looking for something physical, material or structural to be healed or transformed—and, instead, continue to rest, relax, bathe in, and have confidence in the spiritual reality happening in us, our consciousness is clear, like a window, for the whole and healthy corporeal sense of God to be palpably experienced.

Our corporeal sense becomes full of life as spirit is experienced as the one reality. We have a corporeal sense of the spiritual substance and form our body truly is. As long as we know this truth and maintain a conscious state of spiritual oneness, and expect only *spiritual* harmony, *spiritual* health and vitality, then we only have to behold how quickly that spiritual fulfillment becomes evident corporeally (as that which we previously believed to be mental, physical or material).

Nothing is mental, physical or material; all is spirit and spiritual.

PROSPERITY

The same is true when it comes to supply, wealth, success, prosperity. Realize that oneness itself *is* wealth. Oneness itself is the only existent form; and because form is God, which is infinite and omnipresent, all form is infinite and omnipresent.

When we attain and then bathe in a conscious state of oneness, *letting oneness itself fulfill* our senses, we are fulfilling our world with infinite and omnipresent forms and activities of wealth.

The filling of our senses with oneness *is itself* the filling of our world with wealth and success. A conscious state of oneness is the one actuality, the only tangibility, the one reality, the one and practical experience—the one practical wealth "within" and "without."

If we still believe that something "outer" needs to be satisfied, we are still expecting amiss: we are still praying amiss, seeking amiss, hoping amiss, and even resting amiss. "Ye ask, and receive not, because ye ask amiss."

To paraphrase: Ye seek, meditate and sit in silence, and receive not, because ye seek, meditate and sit in silence amiss. This is the only reason we do not experience our health, our wealth, our harmony, our peace, our loving relationship, our joy, our freedom.

But as we know that God is all (and that the experience of God is the experience of conscious oneness) and we are satisfied with the peace of oneness filling our senses "within" and "without," we discover our life filled with the abundant forms of wealth, opportunity and successful activity.

As we know that wealth in all its form—make sure you hear the singular: wealth in all its *form,* infinite and omnipresent—is oneness itself, spirit itself, and that none "else" is; and as we lift into oneness, sit in oneness, and *there* rest and relax, and behold oneness happening as and throughout us; and as we realize that that "happening" *is* the infinity of wealth in all its form, tangibly experienced, we are fulfilled. Our "demonstration" is complete. We have received our wealth. Our entire universe is full of the presence and activity of wealth.

There is no "other" activity, form or presence of wealth; nothing "else" has to happen; there isn't an "outer" which an "inner" has to influence and fulfill as "matter," something God is not. Wealth is one, and *has been fully evidenced* the moment oneness is felt happening. Just do not make "two" of it. Do not make an "outer" different from an "inner." Make the fulfillment of oneness your all-of-all.

Realize that staying in oneness, never hoping for material wealth (because there is not any) but seeking only the awareness of the infinite and omnipresent spiritual wealth, evidences the corporeal sense of wealth.

As we regularly re-experience the infinity and omnipresence of the one wealth, we only have to watch the immediacy of the corporeal sense of it fill our experience. The infinite form of God is ever-present, and as we know it, seek it, and let it reveal itself to us in our silence and transparency of being, our experience is filled with the boundless forms of "material" wealth, success and prosperity the world has.

The one wealth is experienced as corporeal wealth in limitless and unconditional forms, as the need fulfilled, whatever the need may be. It could be money, food, clothing, home, help, direction, idea, innovation, new customers or students; it could be that we feel the impulse to call somebody and that person turns out to be, in one way or another, our fulfillment of this moment, and we his. It could be that a large order is received "out of the blue" for our product, service or treatment. It could be that someone walks through the door with a handsome offer to buy our business or to offer us a lucrative position in theirs.

In any of an infinite variety of ways the one wealth is infallibly experienced. It is the fulfillment of every step of our experience, of our every activity, place and condition, no matter what the form of it looks like.

We have to stop thinking in terms of oneness "and" dollars, oneness "and" customers, clients, patients, students; oneness "and" avenues, methods and vehicles as being financial fulfillment. There is no "vehicle" but God itself. God is "both" the vehicle and the demonstration—self-complete, self-contained and self-evident fulfillment of all.

We have to lose all belief in "material" wealth, avenues, activities, causes and effects, time and space, results. There is no truth to these appearances. Only oneness is; therefore only oneness is true. Oneness itself is the wealth of all form—the infinite and omnipresent wealth, the *only* real and practical wealth.

THE IMAGE OF WEALTH

There is no form but the *one.* Oneness itself is all form. What appears as a dollar is not an entity in and of its own self but an image. What the image truly is is the infinity and omnipresence of the one form. When we realize this and live by it instead of by appearance, we find ourselves with an unconditional abundance of wealthy and prosperous form fulfilling every day, demand, and circumstance. But if we believe dollars or other forms of abundance to be real in and of their own selves, we block from our sense the infinity and omnipresence of the one form which *is,* and fills every nook and cranny of our world. "The earth is full of the goodness of God."

Even though all around us exists limitless and unconditional wealth in actual form, we cannot see it. We throw a cloud over the perfectly visible and tangible abundance that fills our world. But when we know and expect only the one form of wealth fulfillment, we very quickly *have* an overflowing sufficiency of dollars and all other forms of prosperity fulfilling our every step.

LOVE AND RELATIONSHIP

The discovery of our fulfilling love and relationship, family, companion, colleague and neighbor is the discovery of God, oneness, spirit itself being all that love is. To discover the truth of individual being, the truth of lover, spouse or partner, family, customer, patient, student, colleague and neighbor forget about what is believed about him or her.

Lift up into an awareness of the one being you know he truly is—God, spirit. Once you have attained a conscious state of oneness you have his truth. The truth of being fills your senses. If you can rest there, and in your rest *behold* the oneness of being filling your mind, *being* your awareness, you are able to look out at people and experience their truth, their love, their light, their harmony and friendliness.

It does not necessarily mean that *they* will experience their truth, at least not beyond the few moments or minutes they remain in your consciousness. Family, friends, close students and neighbors who remain in your consciousness, by the degree they are open, are eventually released from belief and discover their freedom, at least partially. You will watch people soften, become lighter, more agreeable, more joyous, more free from the "human" burdens they carry around.

People have to be at least somewhat spiritually receptive. If they are, sooner or later they experience a measure of their freedom in the illumined presence of god-being.

But be careful. "We" have to be rid of the belief in "others" or "otherness." We must not take it upon our shoulders to lift and free others. If we do, we still believe "others" exist; we still believe in God "and." And if we believe that, we will continue to discover that it is impossible to evidence God in or for any of our "ands," our "otherness."

All that matters is that *we* experience the truth of them, which means experiencing *God itself* as all. Then we are the healing balm: the harmonizing, comforting, prospering, pacifying, freeing presence to all perceived beings and conditions. "Where the spirit of the Lord is, there is liberty"—there is life, comfort, abundance, freedom, safety and security.

BUSINESS

To experience the truth of our business or career, our practice or teaching, our church or charity, we go to where it is and what it is, which is oneness. Once we are in a conscious state of oneness, realizing that oneness itself is the only business, the only activity, the only success and prosperity, the only customer, we rest and behold truth "coming through" in all its form.

There is no other form of truth. The one truth in all its form is the experience of oneness happening as and throughout our universe. It is God, spirit "happening" as and throughout us, as all that we perceive. Once we experience that *and once we expect nothing other than spiritual* success, wealth, spiritual business and customer, we *have* it as our business prosperity.

When we truly know that only spirit is, then of course we run to that conscious state of oneness as quickly and as often as we can. We bathe there for longer periods each day and night. Once we bathe there we have the infinity and omnipresence of God as all that we do, and as all its fulfilling wealth.

All business is God-business. "I am about my Father's business." There is none other. When we are consciously aware of this truth, and act as a god rather than as a human, doing god-business rather than material business, we *are,* and *evidence,* the fruits of oneness. We have the infinity and omnipresence of customers, clients, patients or students, and limitless achievement and prosperity right where we are as we live in, and as, and experience a conscious state of oneness.

God is omnipresence and is already where we are. Our entire business activity, success and prosperity, our customers, clients, patients or students are right here in and as oneness—the one business activity, the one prosperity, one customer, client, patient or student, the one success. As we sit and experience conscious oneness happening, we have a success unknown to the world, unlimited in scope, value and growth.

Even if we are the "least in the kingdom" of conscious oneness, our business flourishes beyond the greatest of worldly potential. Do you see that? Even as the least of conscious oneness—even if we believe we are not yet that "good" at lifting into and staying in conscious oneness, but we are able to sit back and rest and relax, and *feel God hap-*

pening—this is sufficient God presence and visibility to behold the most wonderful corporeal success and wealth. Feeling God happening is the key, is the experience, the realization, the demonstration of everything God is and has; the completeness and wholeness, the image and likeness of the one form. Our business, career, teaching, charity, church, our community fair, or garage sale, and even our potato patch, flourish in ways unknown and unknow*able* to human sense.

We each have all the good of God, in all departments of experience, tangibly available to us when we know that only oneness is, and when we never again expect a mental, physical, material, structural, corporeal fulfillment or healing. Nothing mental, physical, material, corporeal exists in God, and because God is the only, none of these exists—*period.*

Only God is, and God is spirit, one. "Besides me there is none else." The real and tangible experience of God as our corporeally sensed world, inclusive of everything in it and of it, *is* the experience of conscious oneness itself and the resting and relaxing in it, beholding God "happening" throughout us, "for us."

"Ye are the temple of the living God" *Let that living God live you.* Let that living God, the living light, form and visibility of truth, live as and throughout your mind, body and world and everything of it.

We cannot remain dimly aware as we stay in even a degree of conscious oneness, letting God be the light of our mind, body and world. Do you believe that your sense of physical and material form can remain dim when you allow God to be the light of your mind and the sense of your experience? Do you believe anything can be discordant, ill, diseased, injured or decrepit in body when we let God live our body for us? Do you believe disease, injustice, insecurity, lack, limitation, poverty, starvation, unhappiness can exist in our world when we let God live our world experience for us? Of course not.

As we let God live for us, all we are left to do is serve the abundant fruits of good we find our world filled with, give them; feed the world with the living forms of God which become ever more evident the more we sit in a conscious state of oneness, simply beholding the kingdom of *I* taking place.

Of course nothing of good is discordant or absent in the kingdom of oneness. Only God is happening and only God is present. And because God and form are one, only God-form, God-activity, God-amount, God-health, God-awareness, God-happiness, God-love, God-purpose and God-fulfillment are true of experience.

In God consciousness, a conscious state of oneness, with no pairs of opposites operating in us (no good versus bad, but God as all and God *already* formed, visible, tangible, manifested and demonstrated), we are free and able to freely give, serve and share the abundant good which fills our lives.

We are free and able, in the most real and practical ways, to heal, feed, *comfort, save and free* all in our individual world, to be "the gods" of all in our experience, to evidence the one true and boundless existence that we *are.*

Indeed, one is what God (good) is, what I am, what all is, and is already where I am.

One. This is the truth, the gift of God, and this is how the gift is made evident "in earth as it is in heaven."

Only God is, therefore only God can.

"Ye are the temple of the living God." *Let the living God live you.*

The "practice of the presence of God" is the practice of *being a conscious state of oneness.*

26933885R00081

Printed in Great Britain
by Amazon